If Lost, Please Return To:

Name:_____

Phone:_____

Email:_____

# Color Test Page

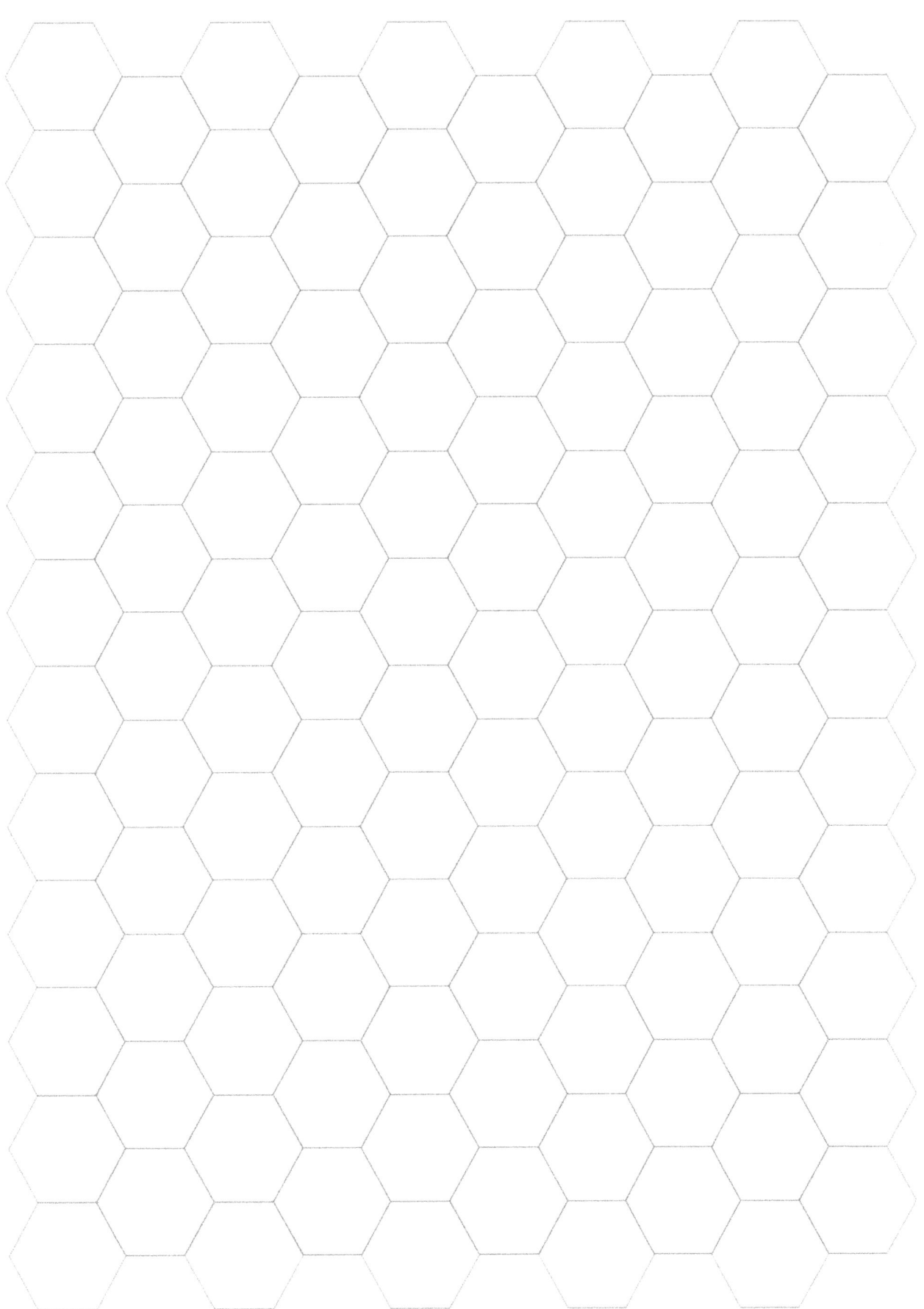

# Color Test Page

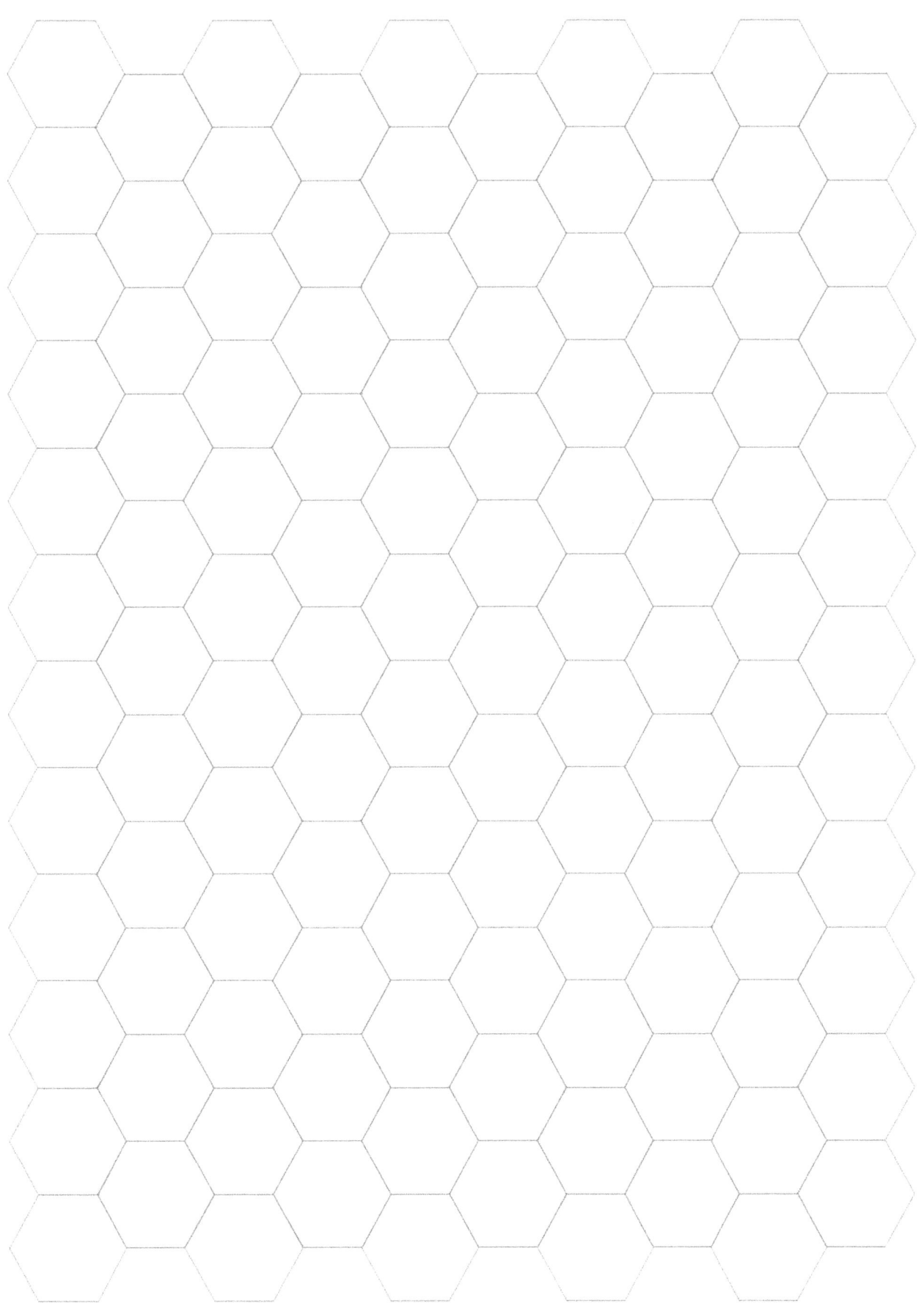

# Color Test Page

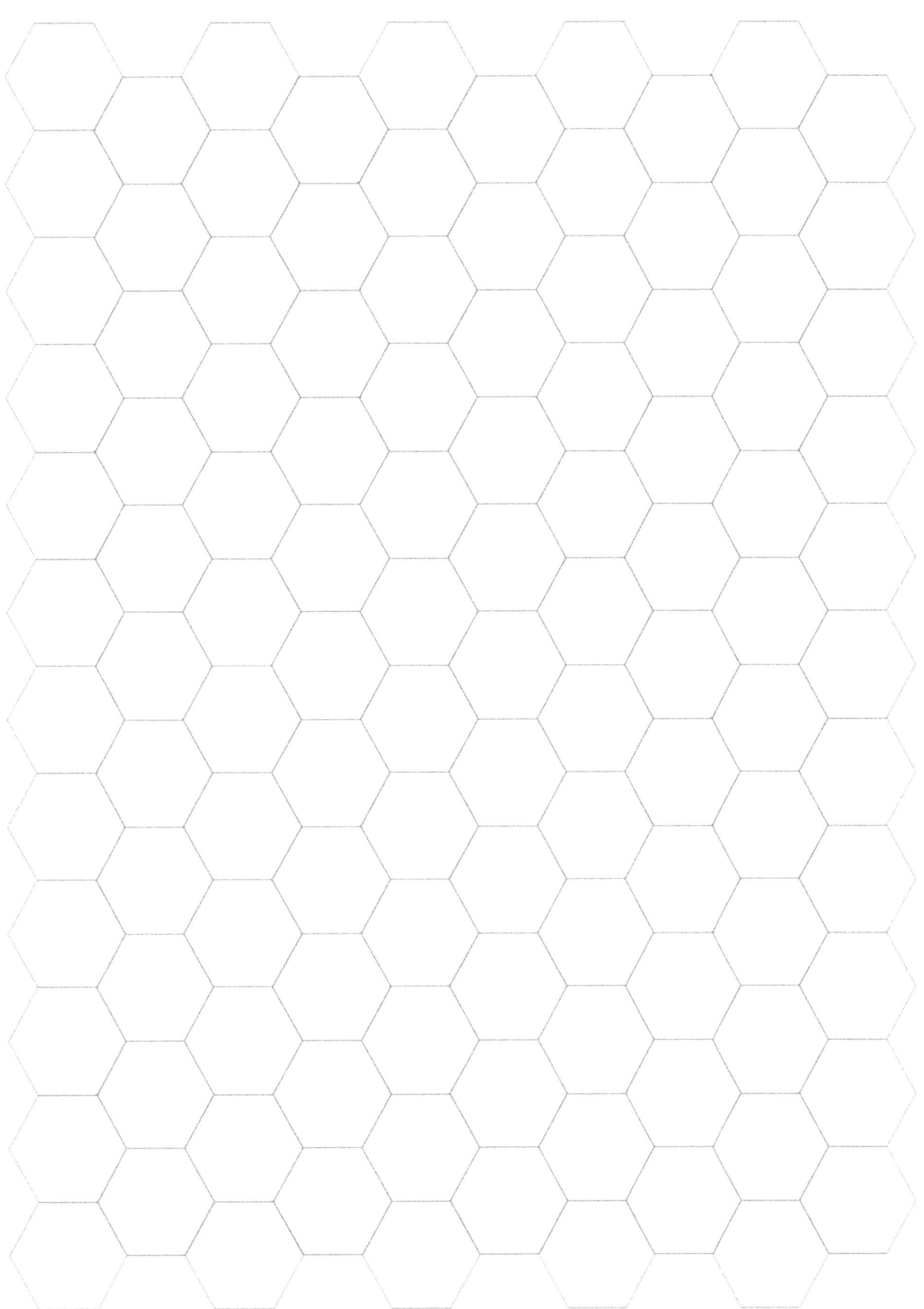

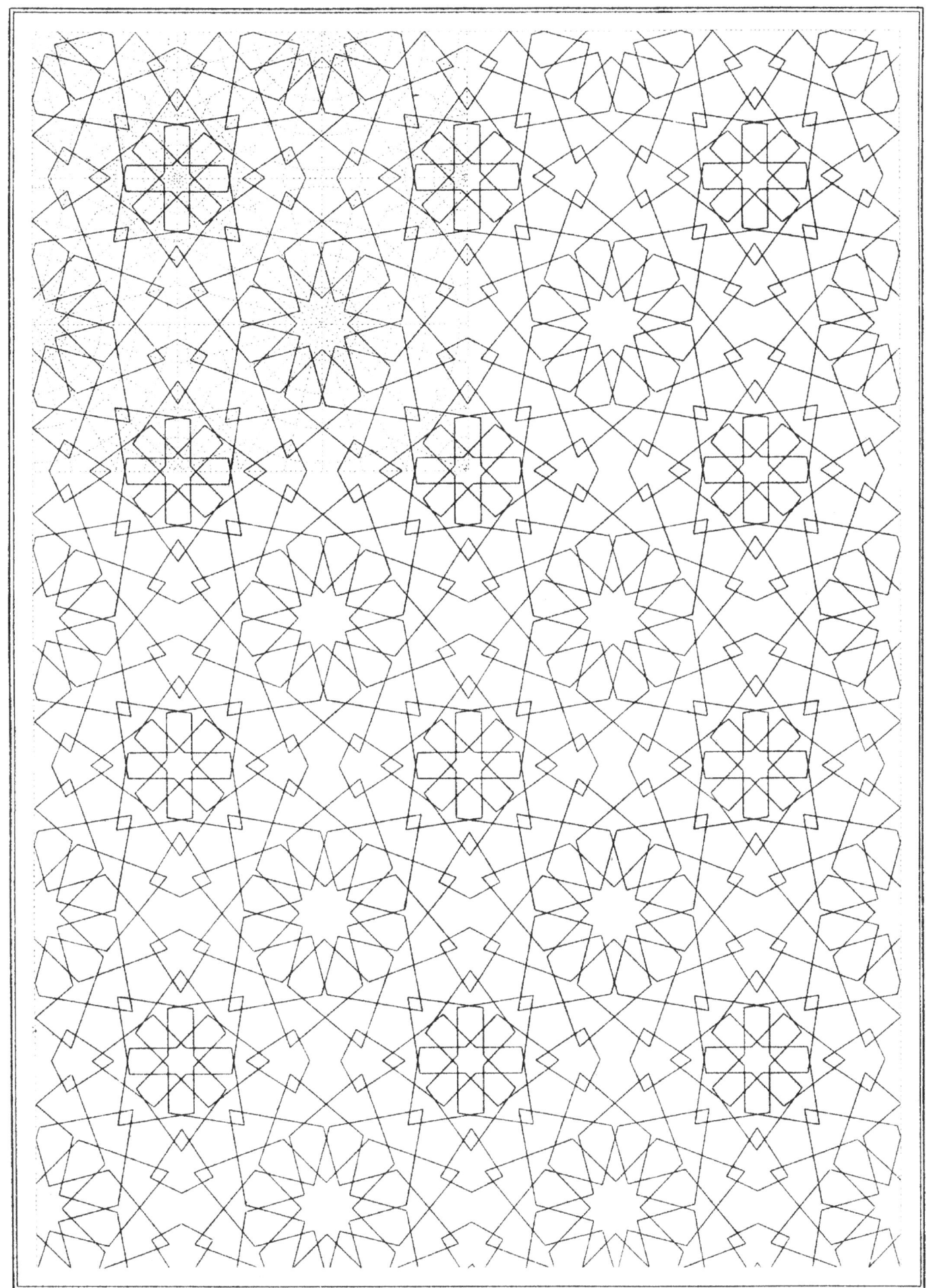

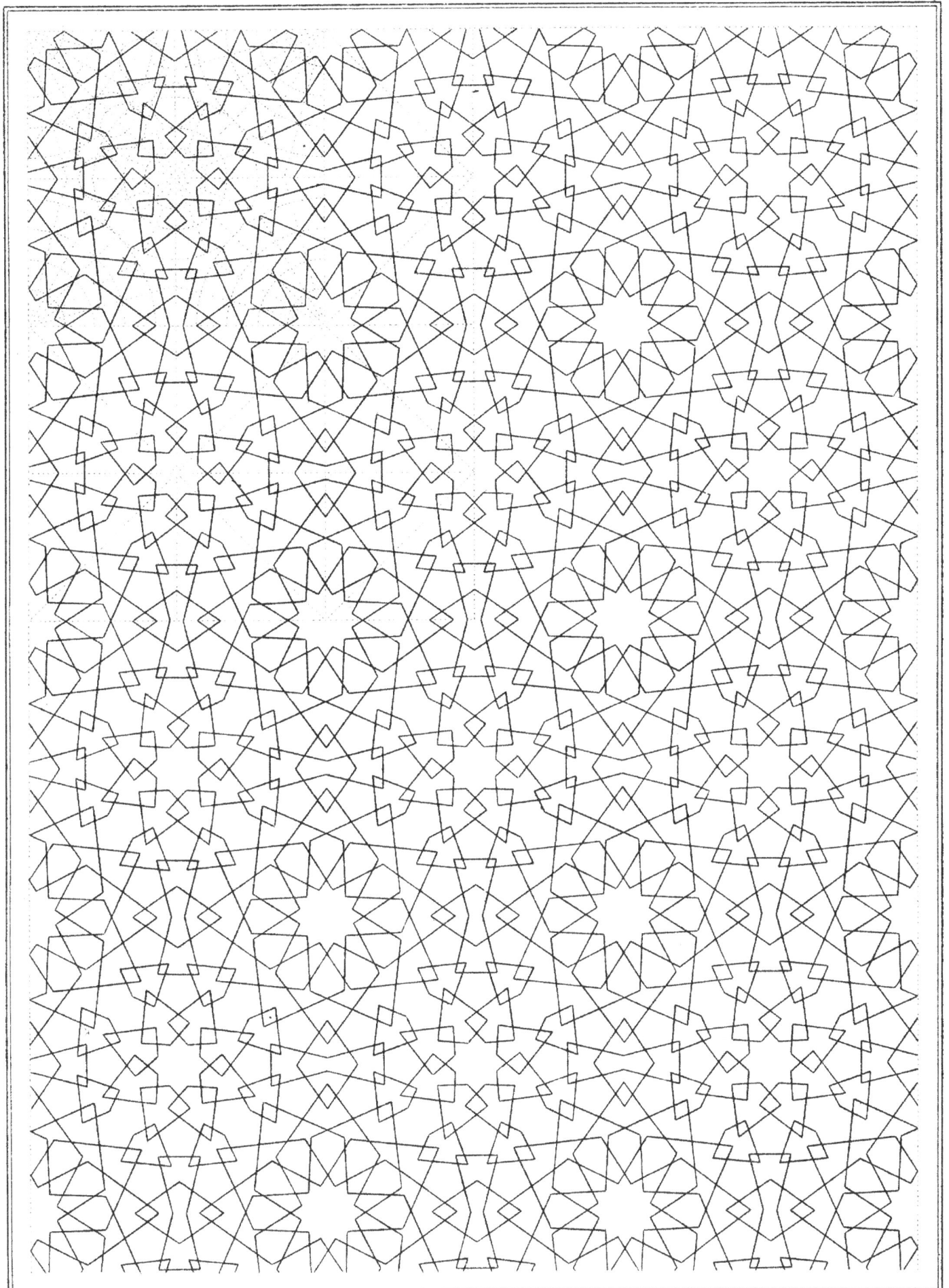

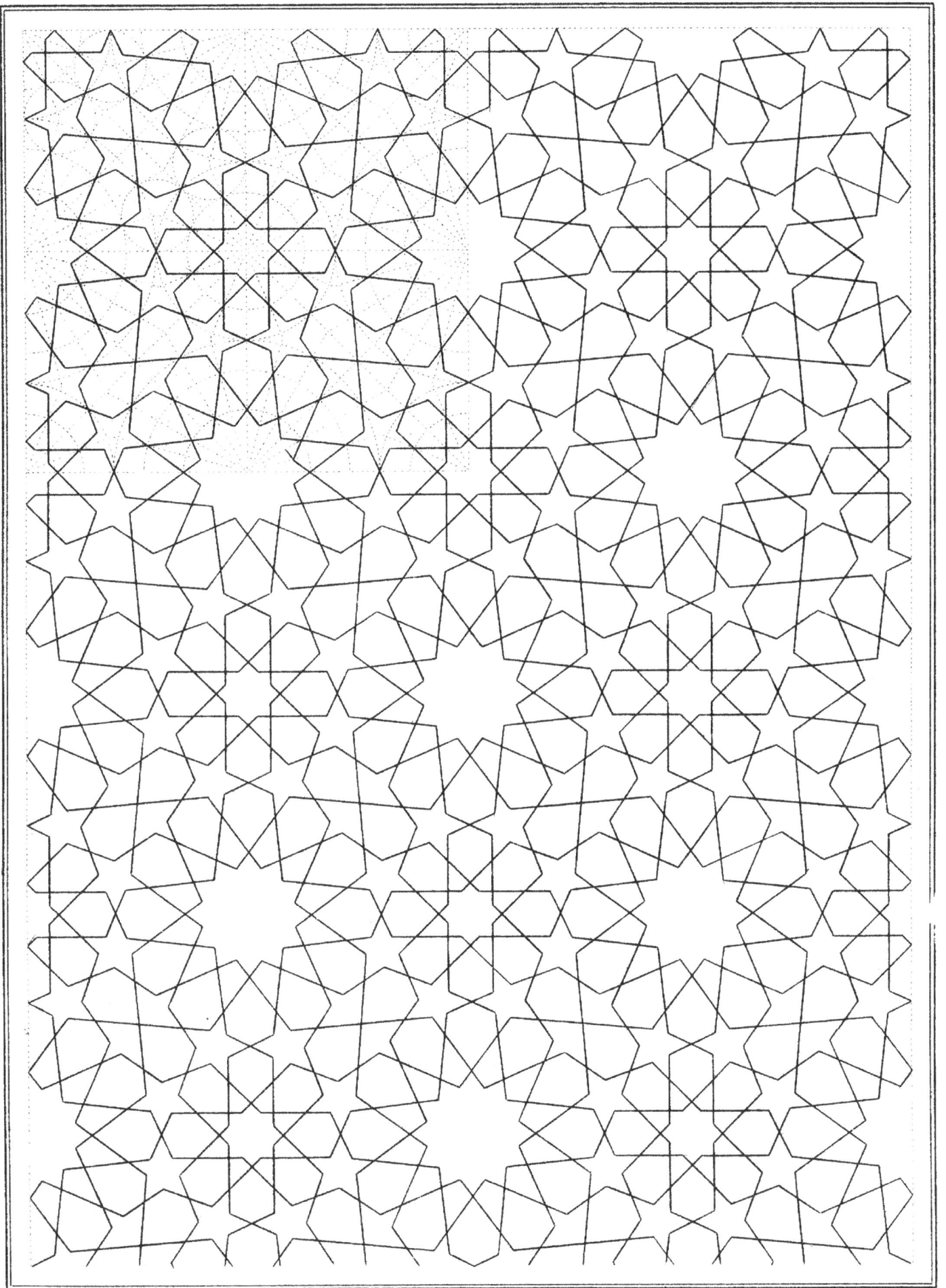

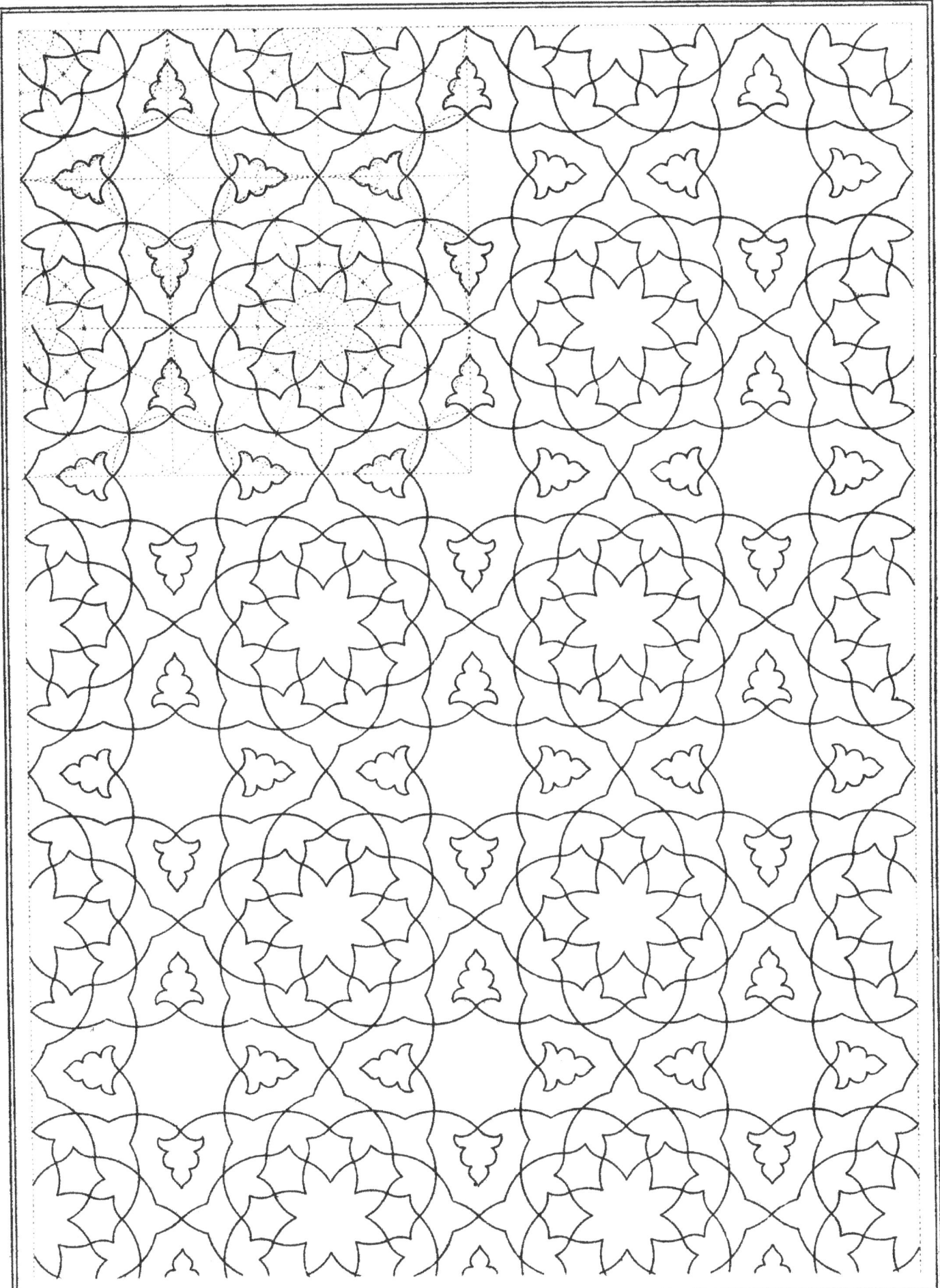

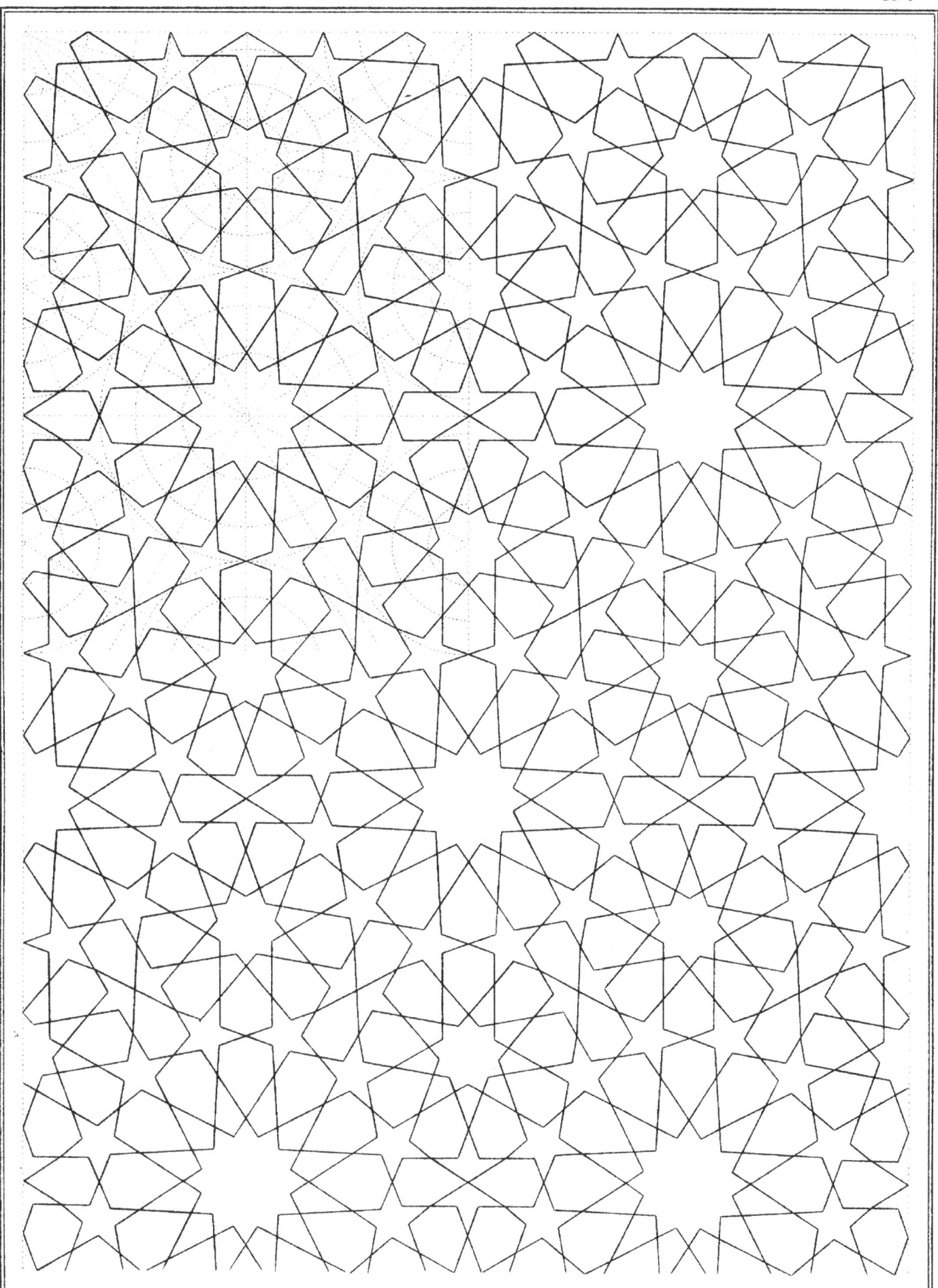

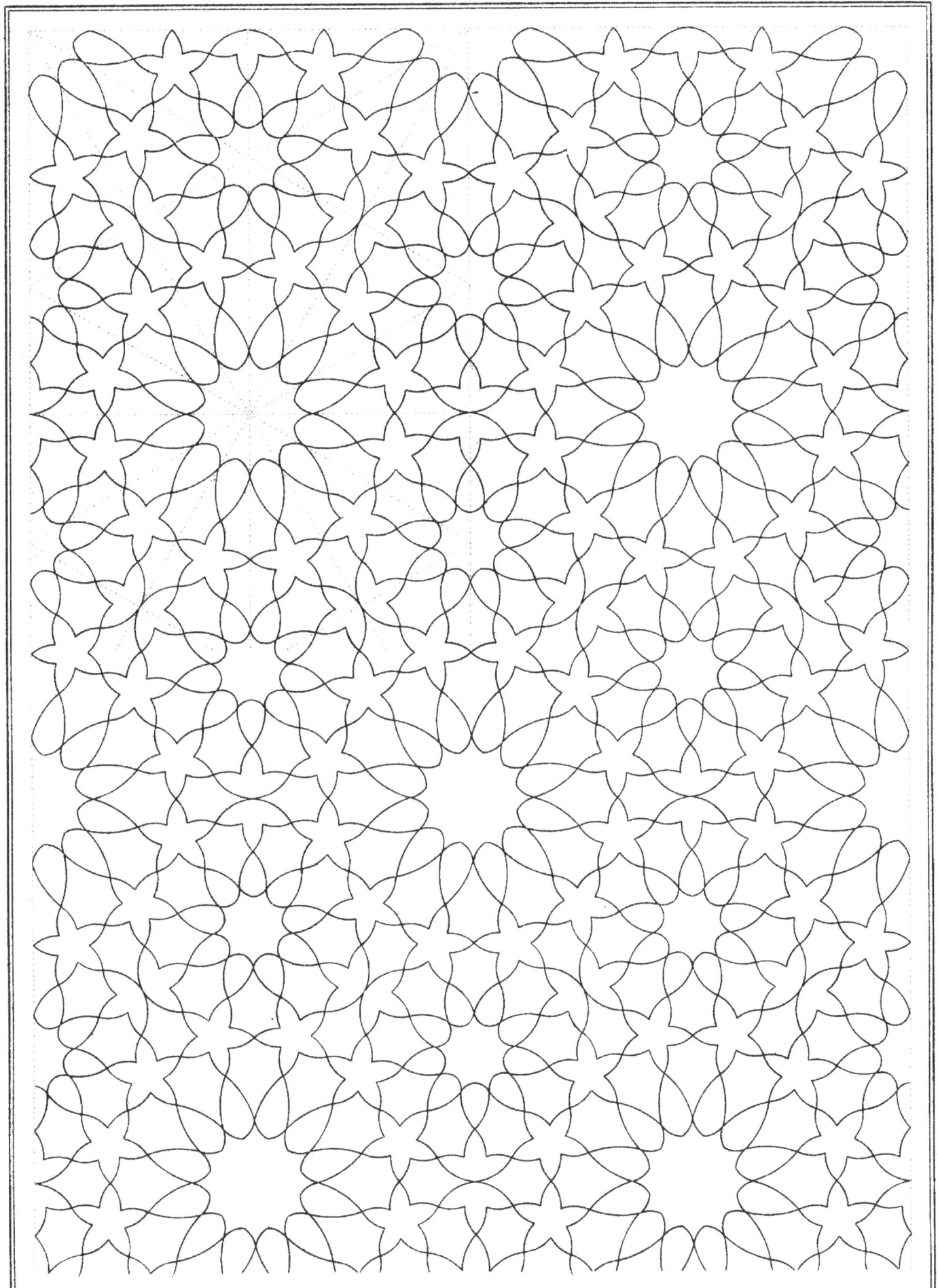

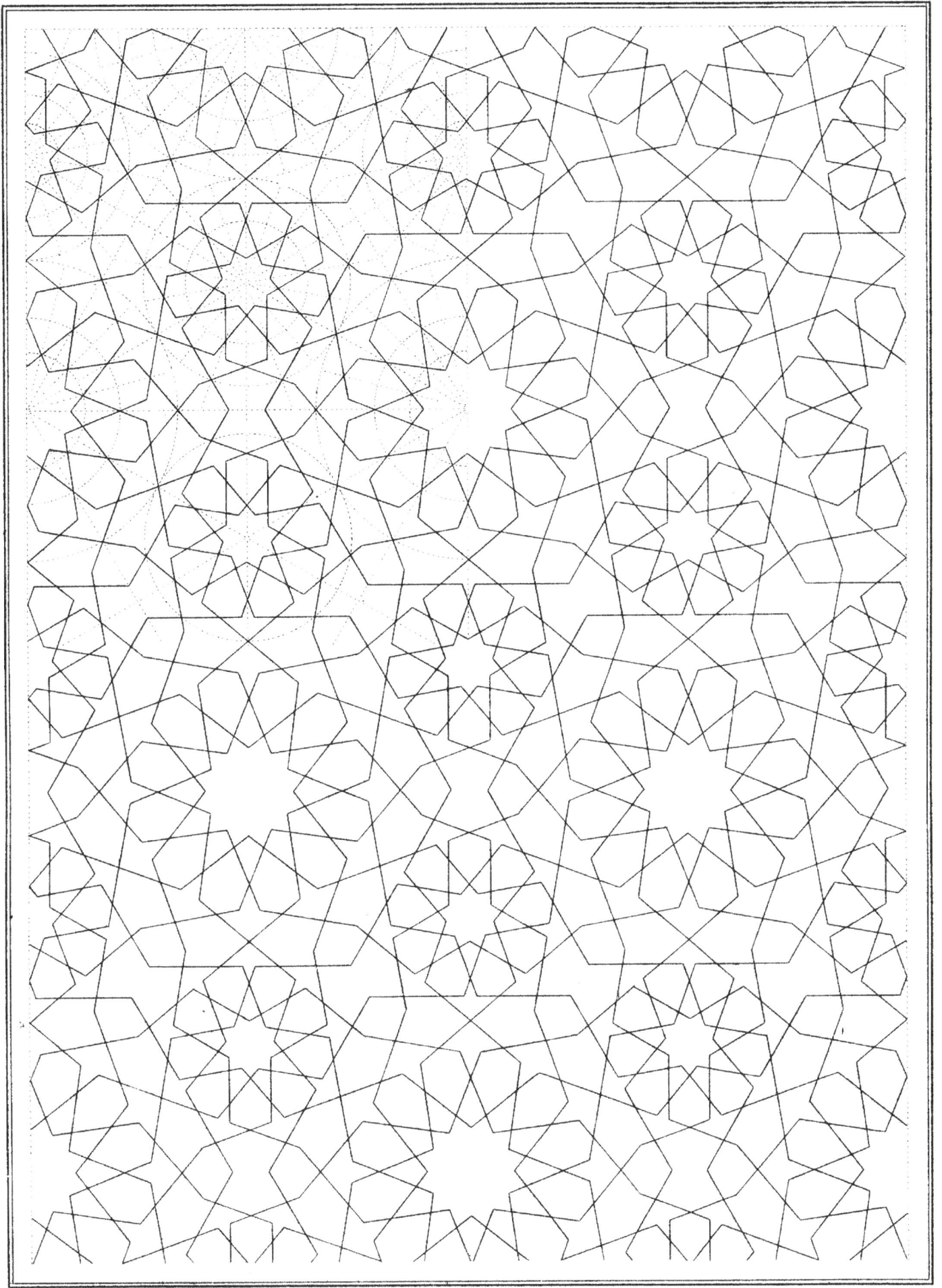

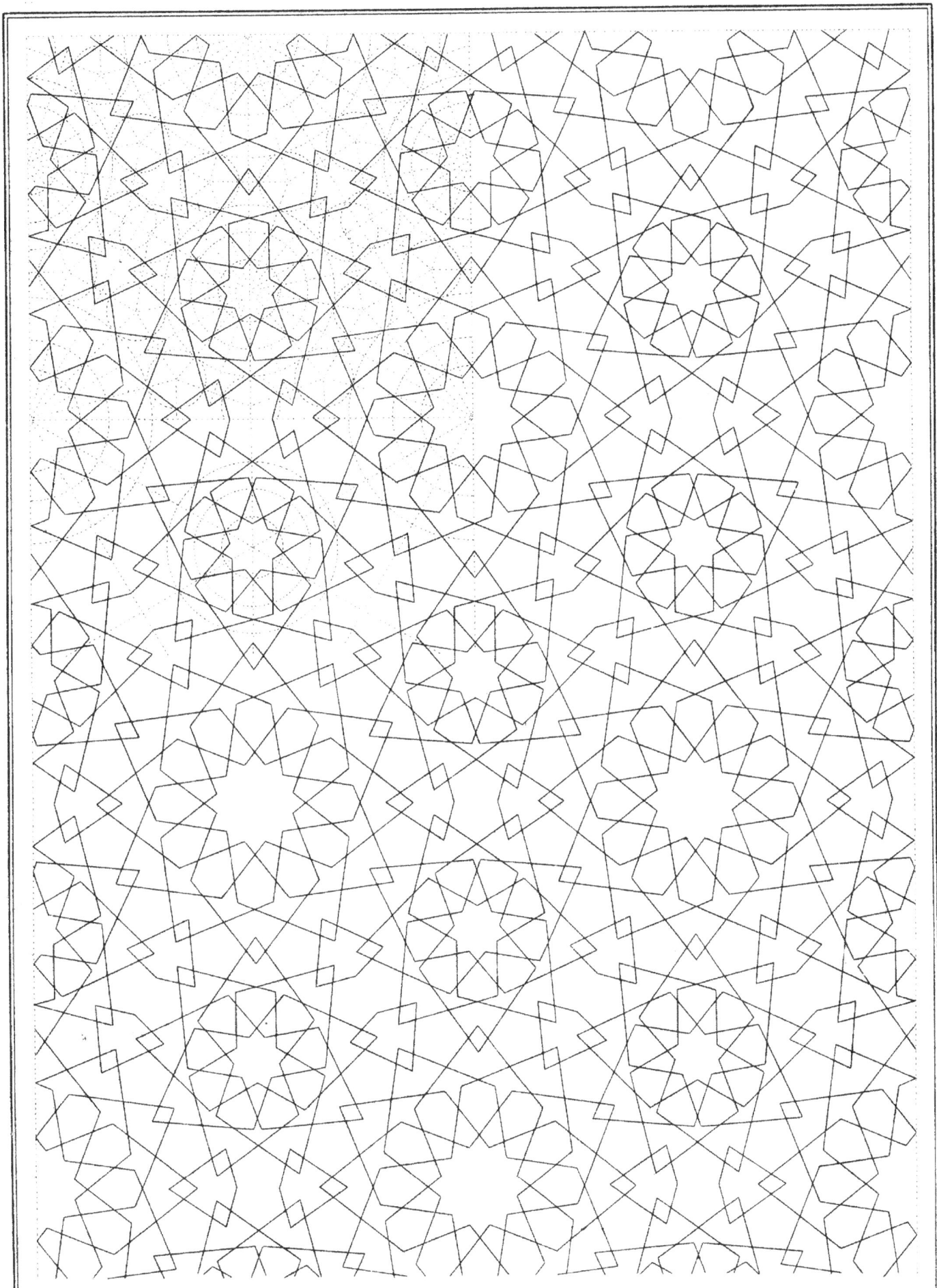

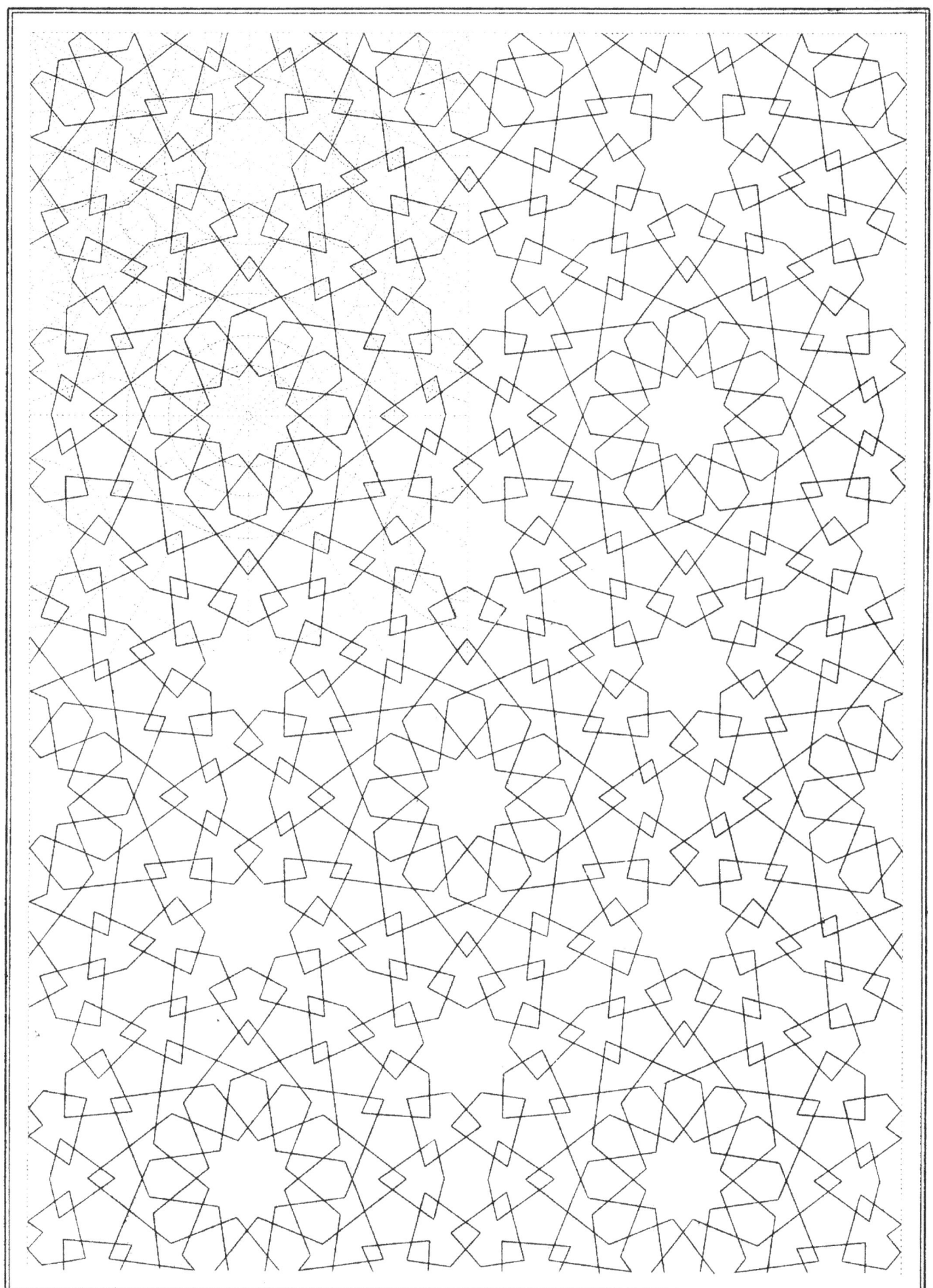

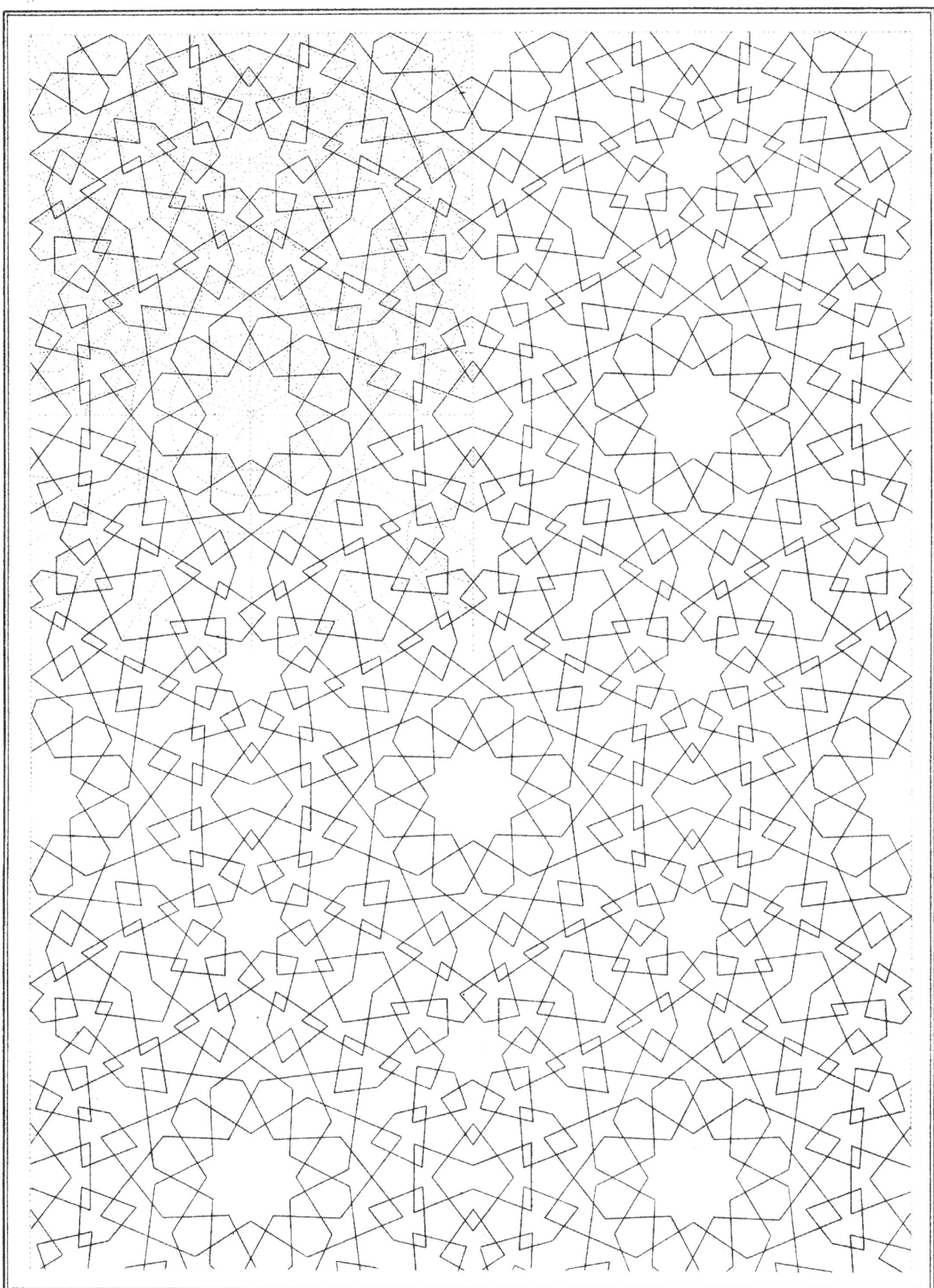

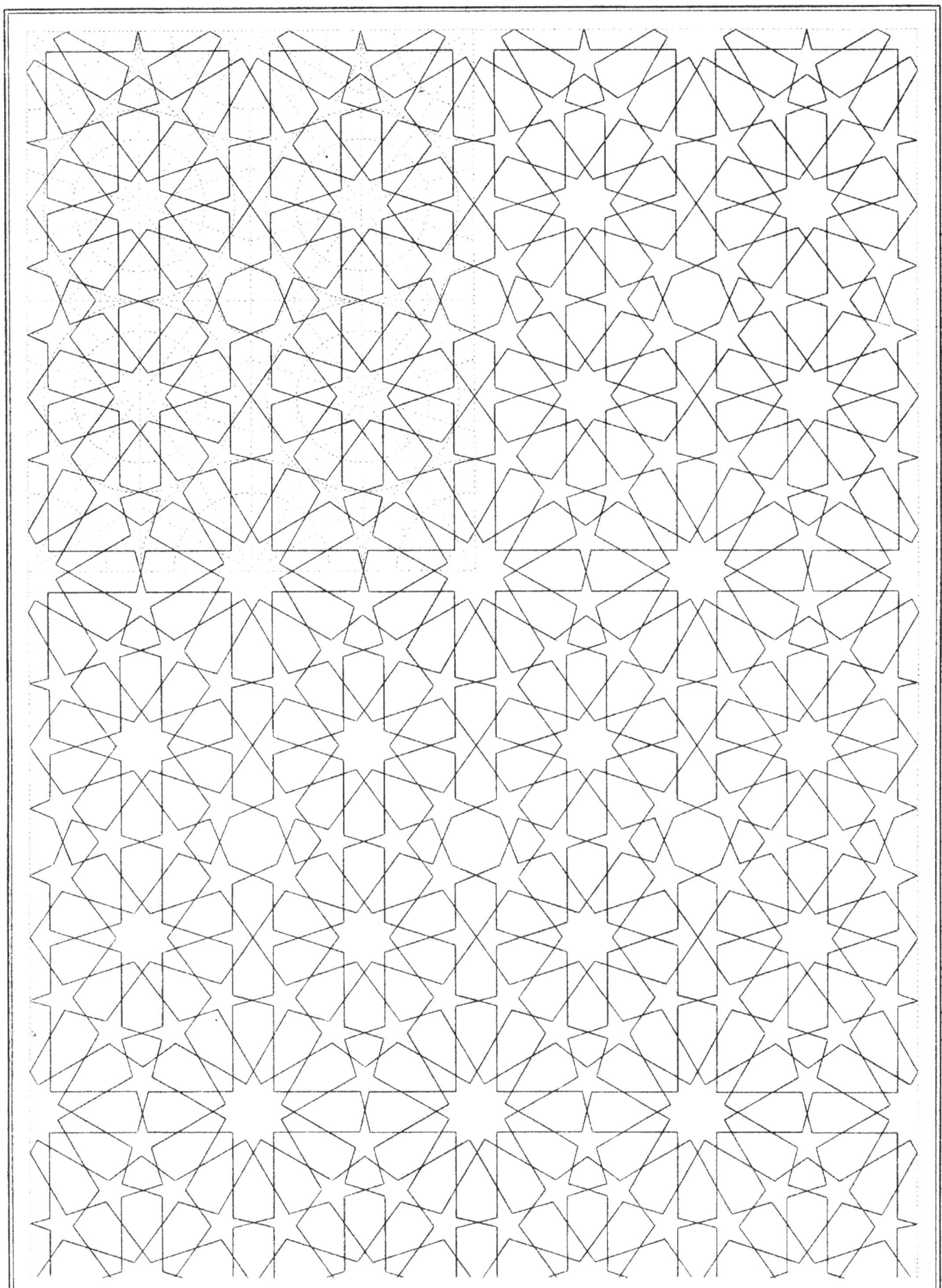

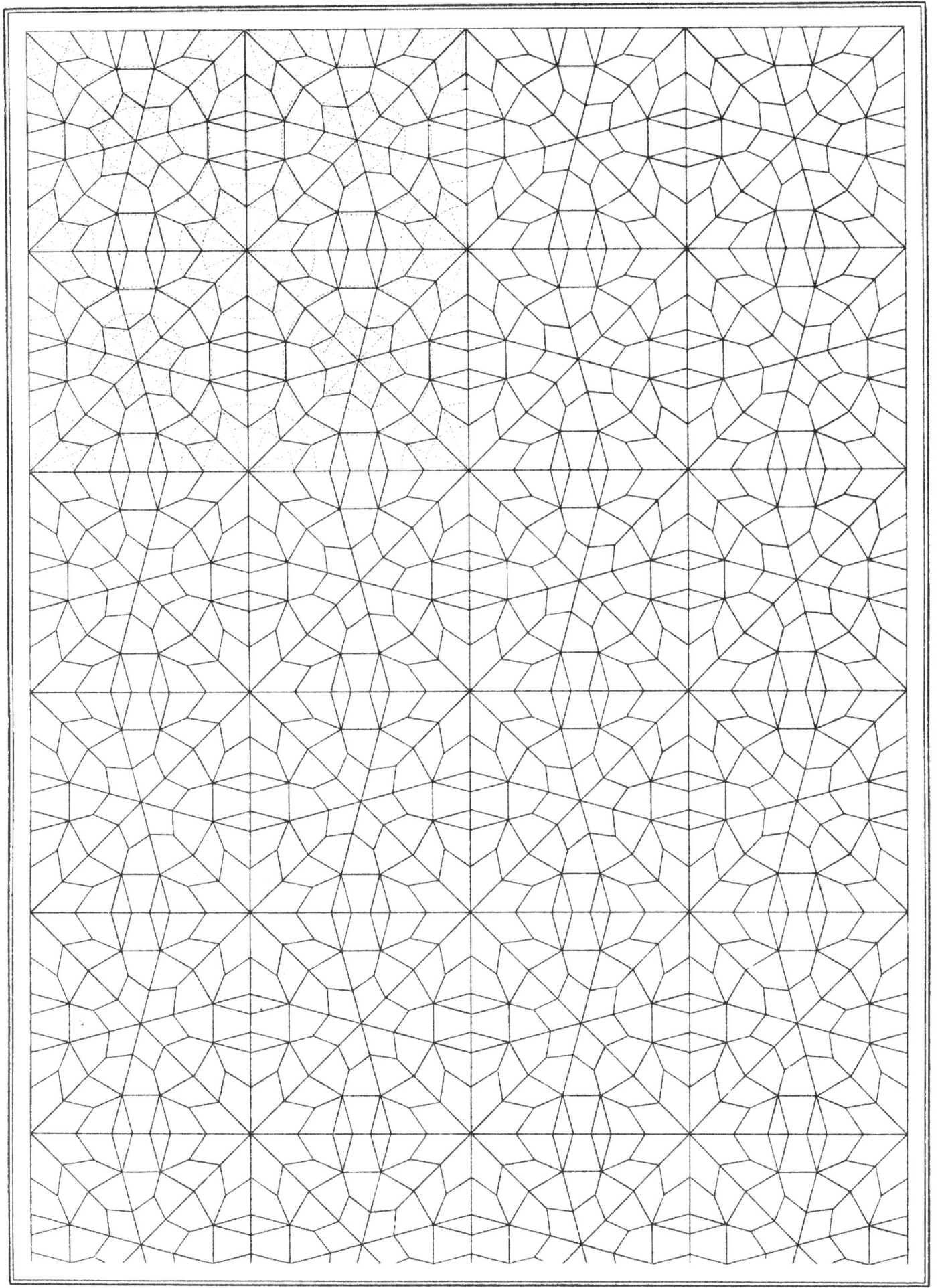

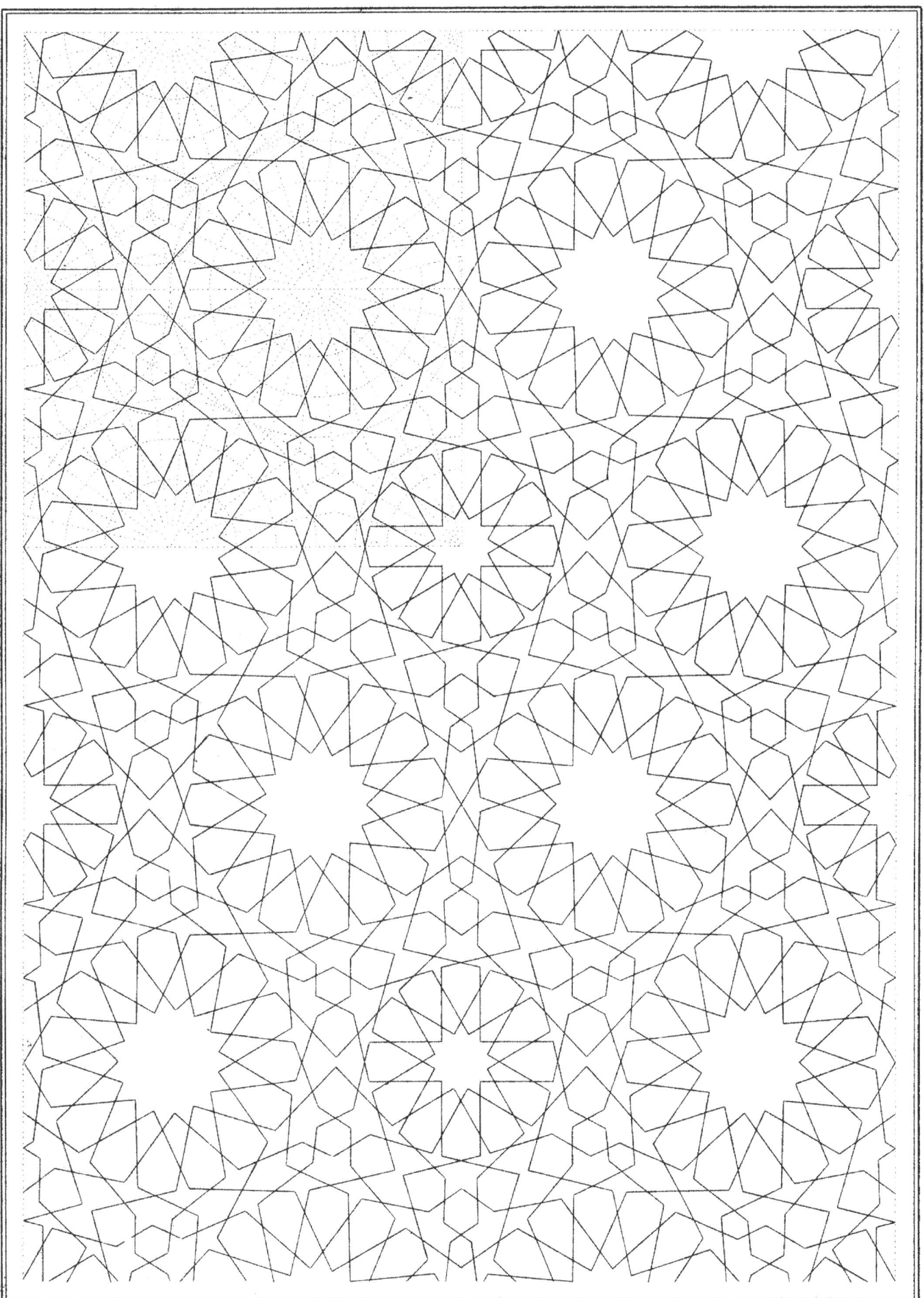

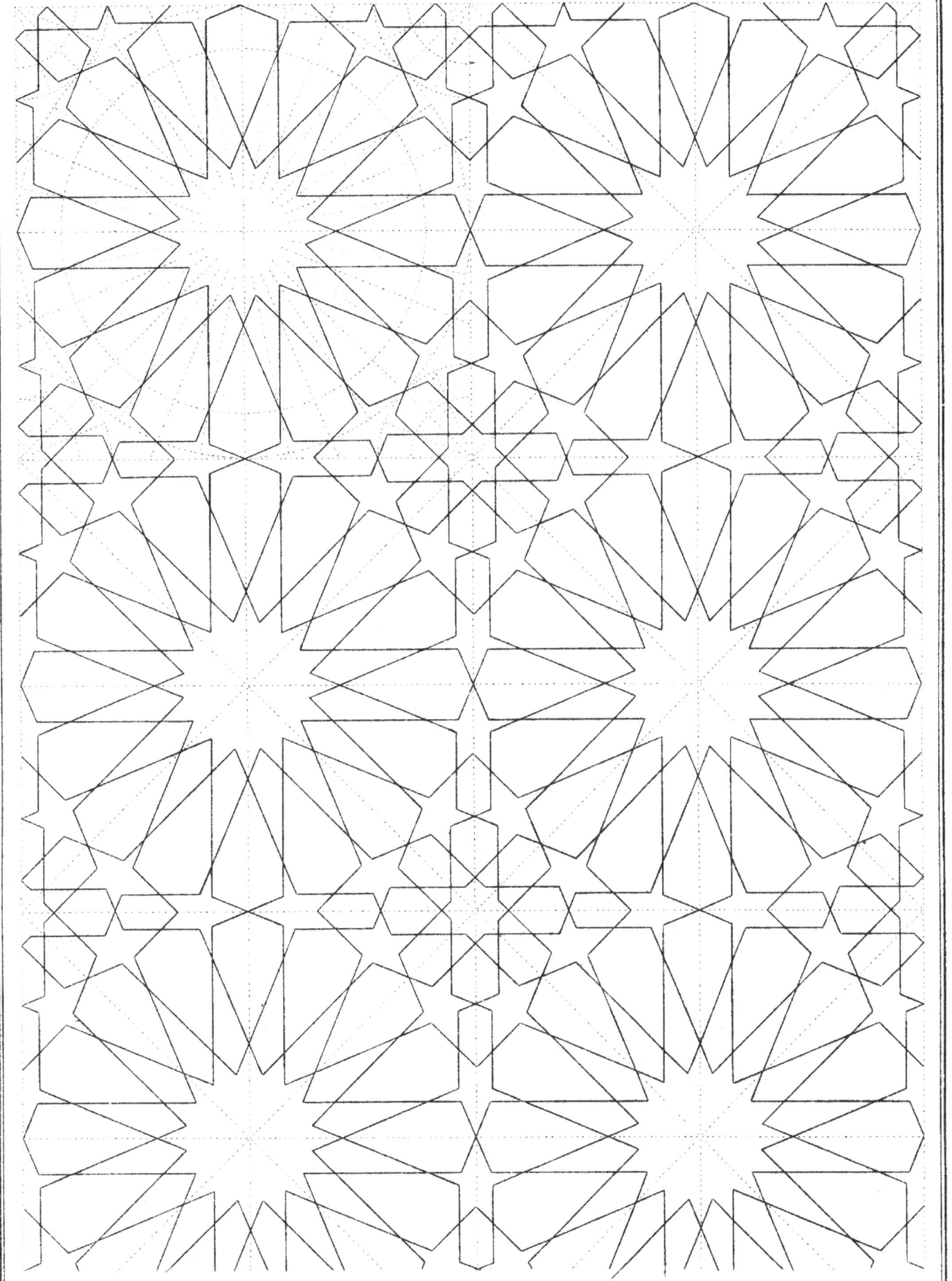

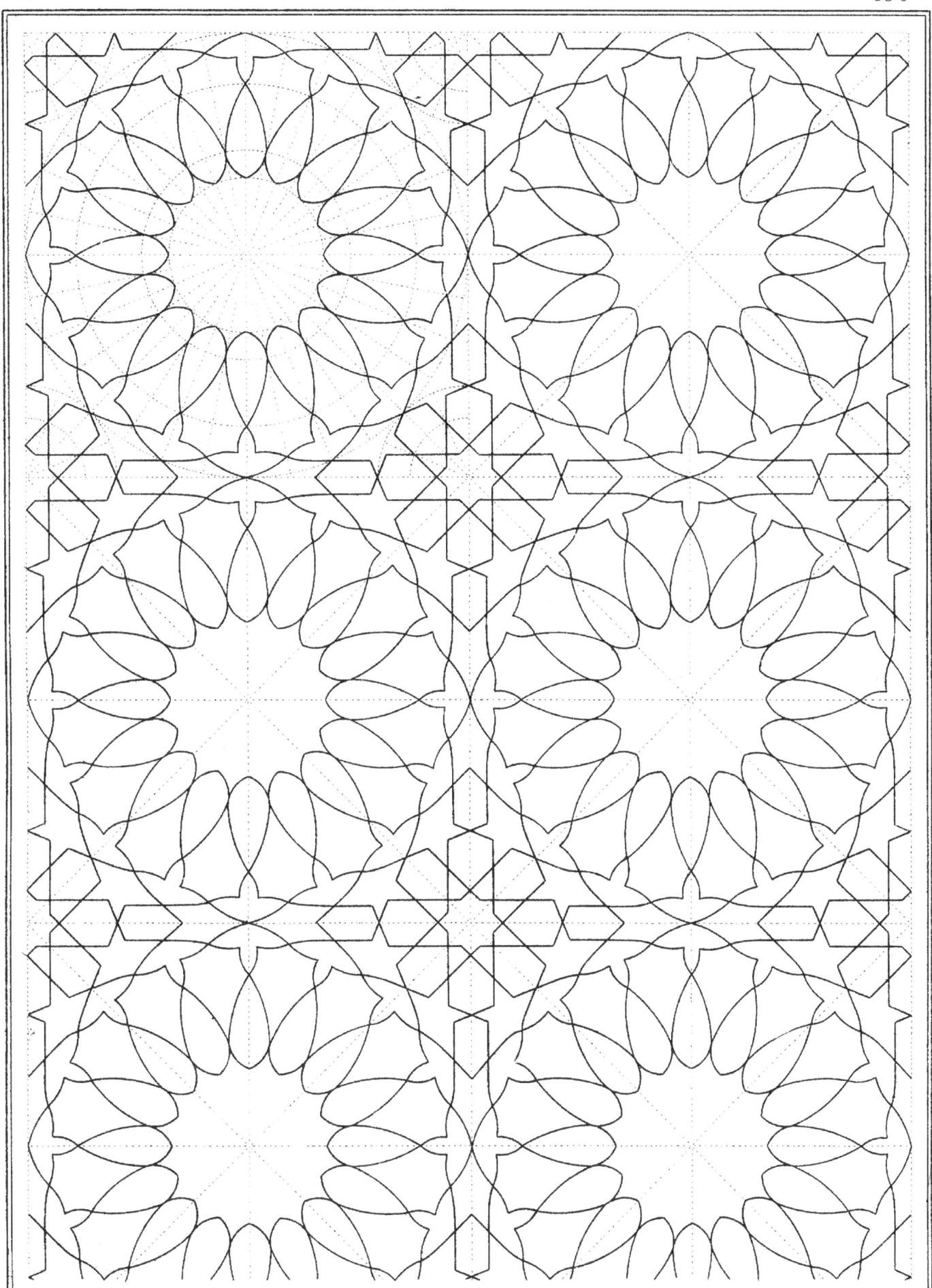

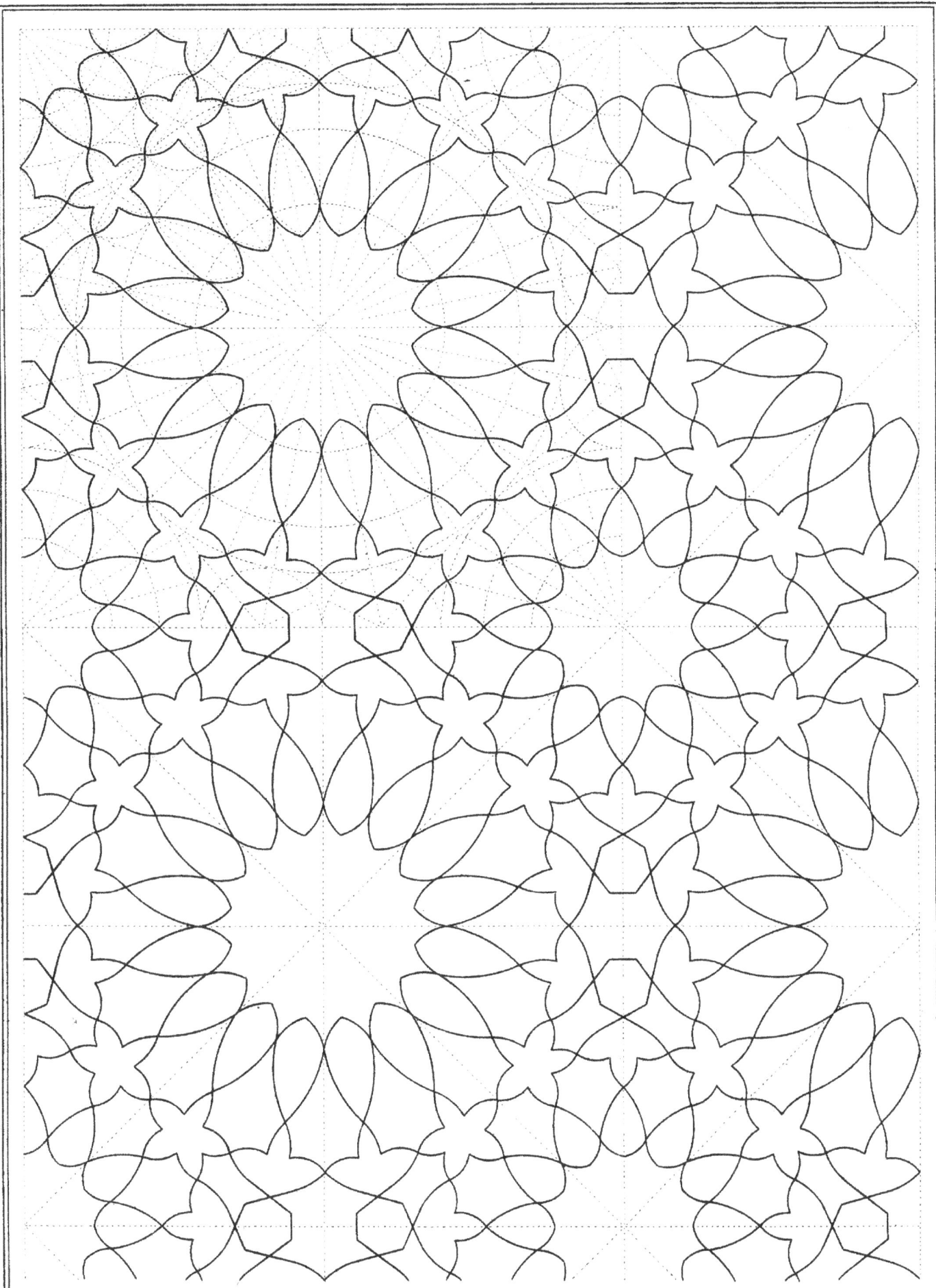

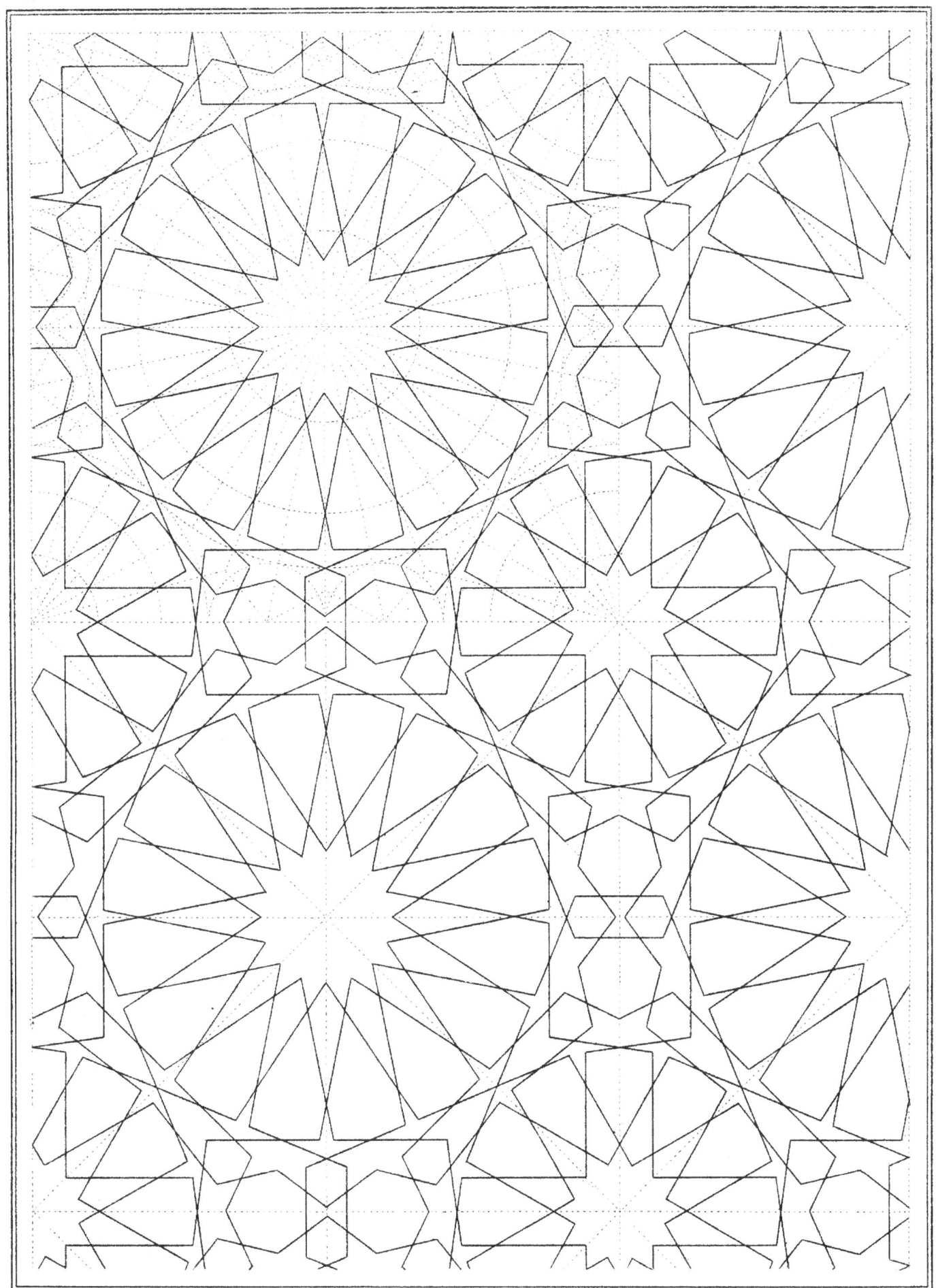

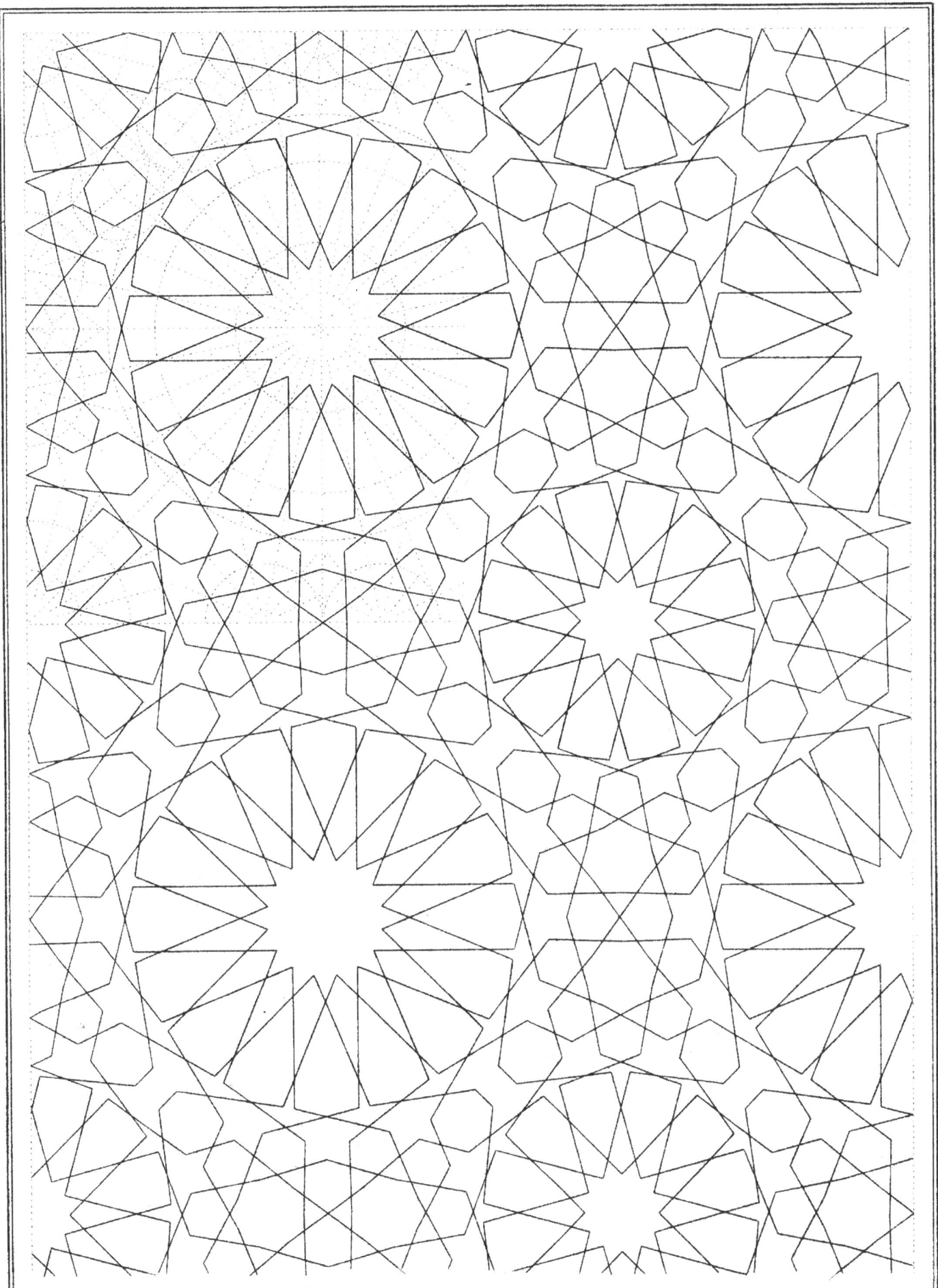

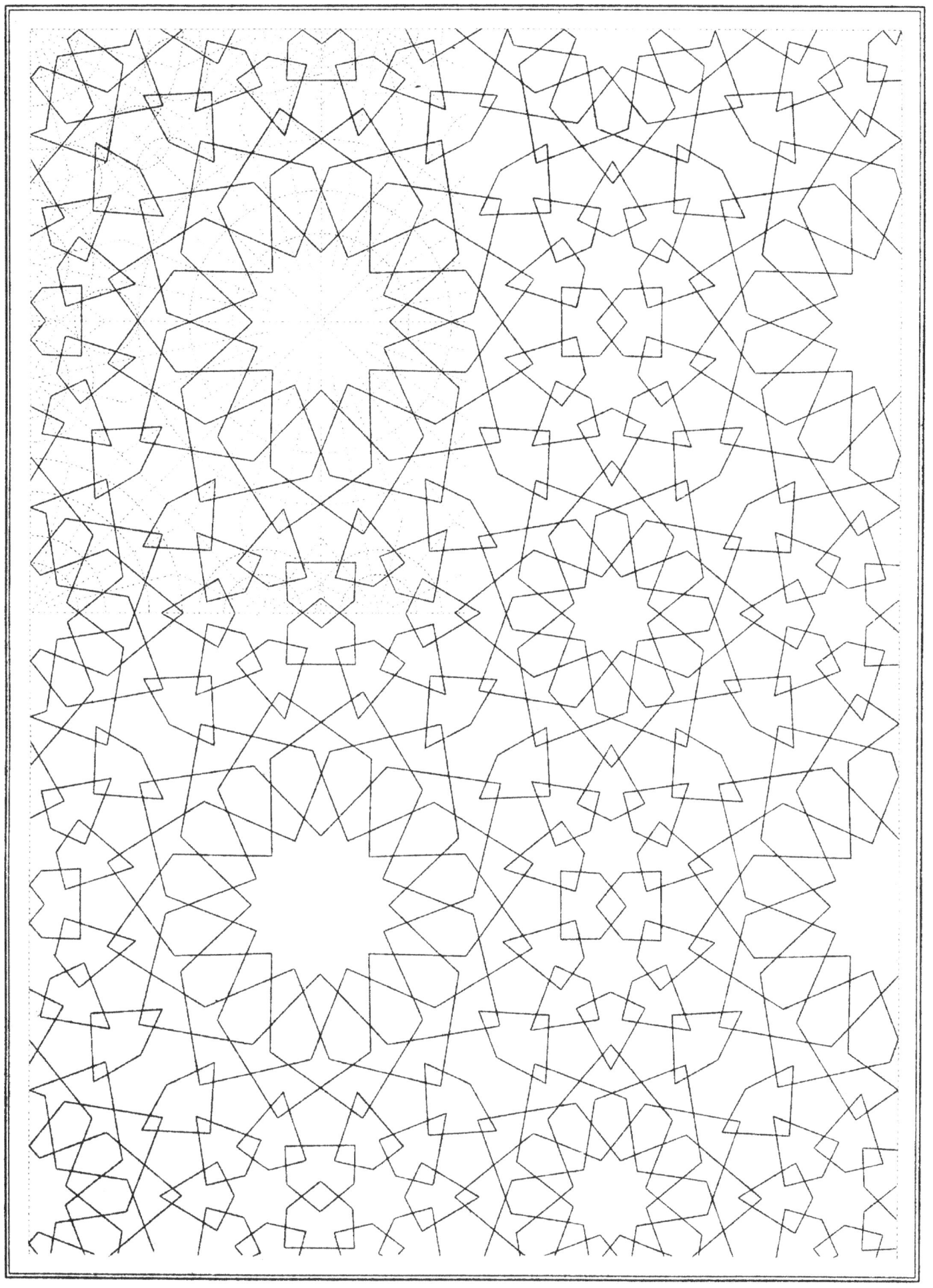

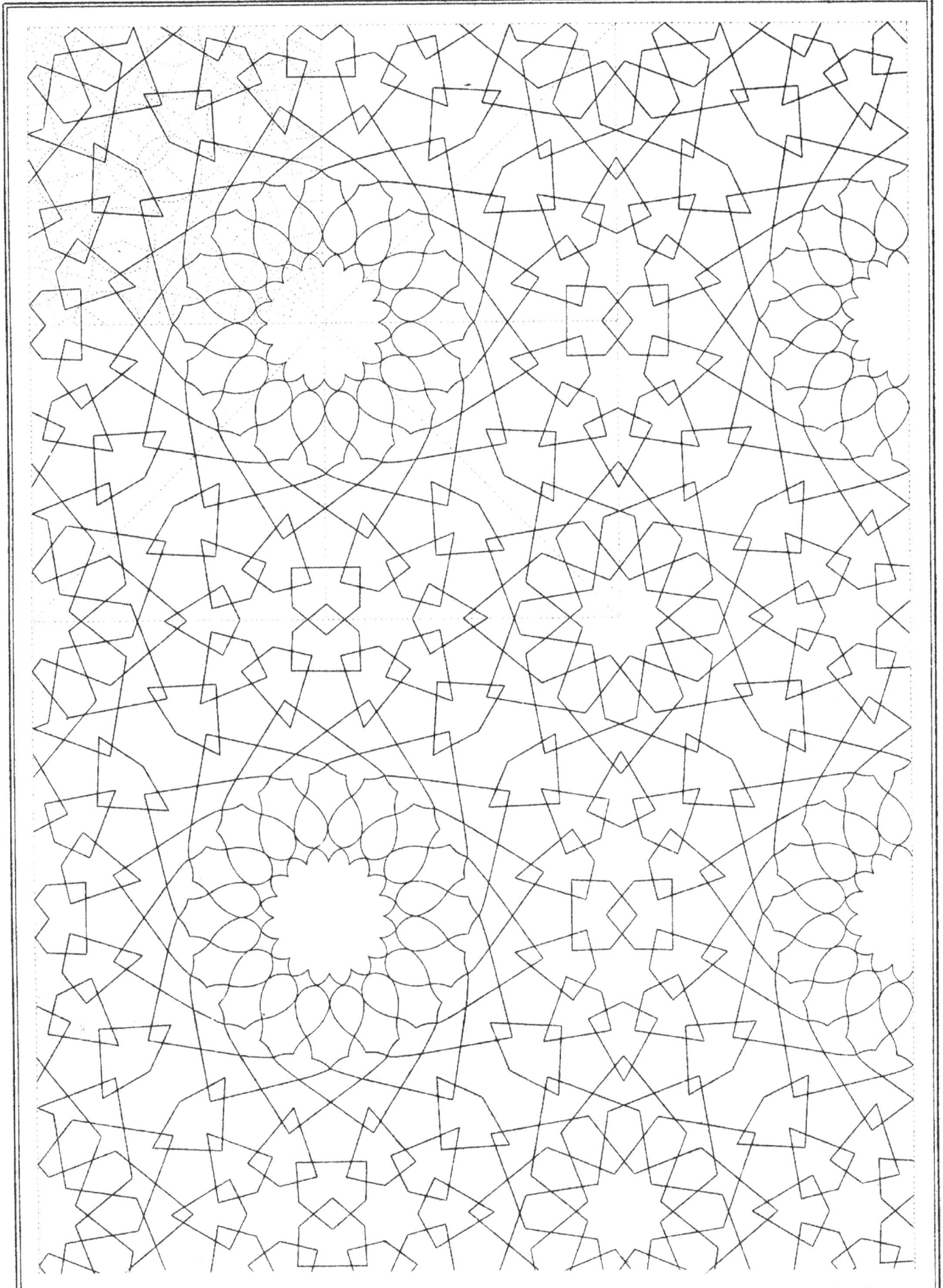

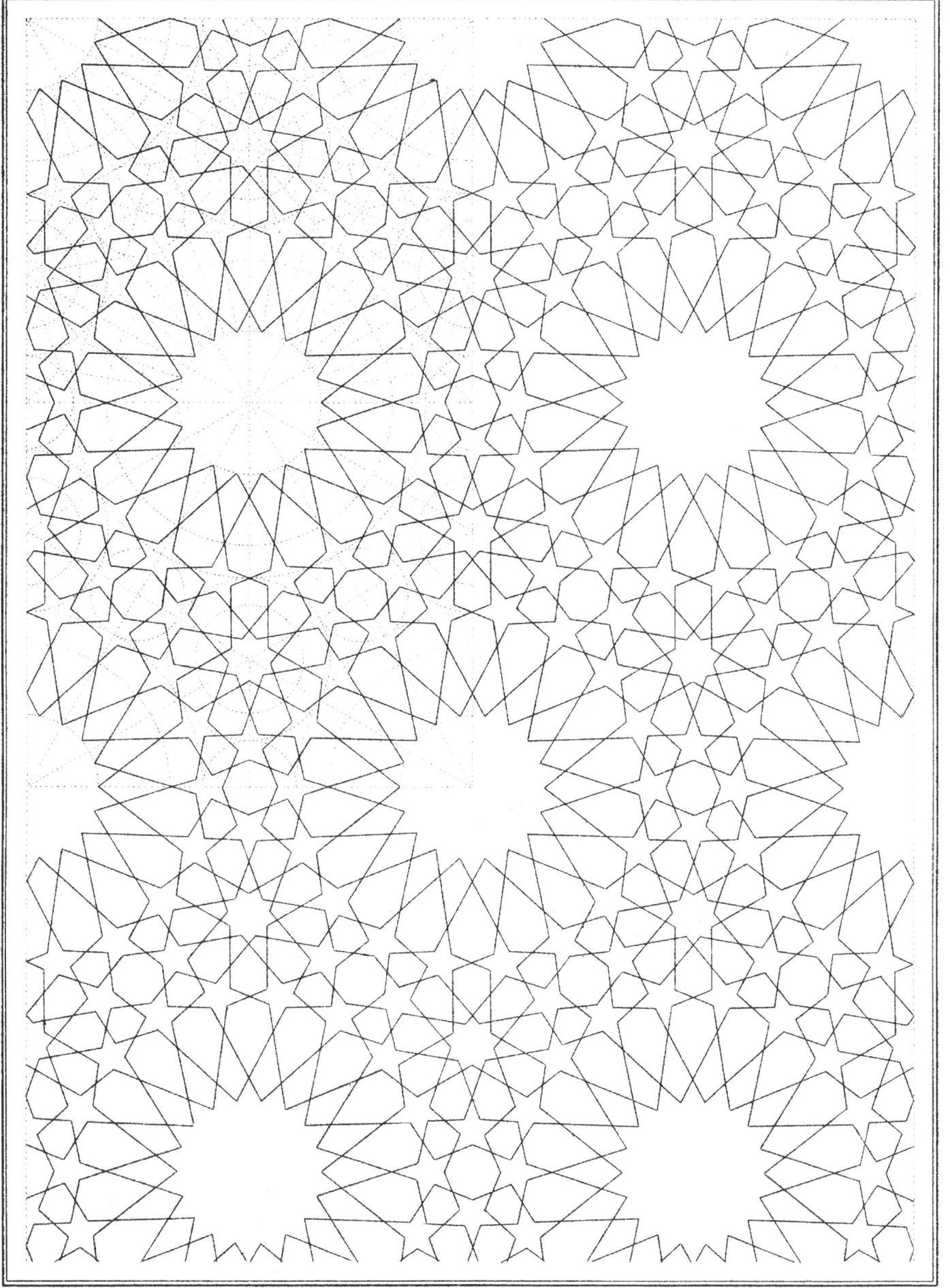

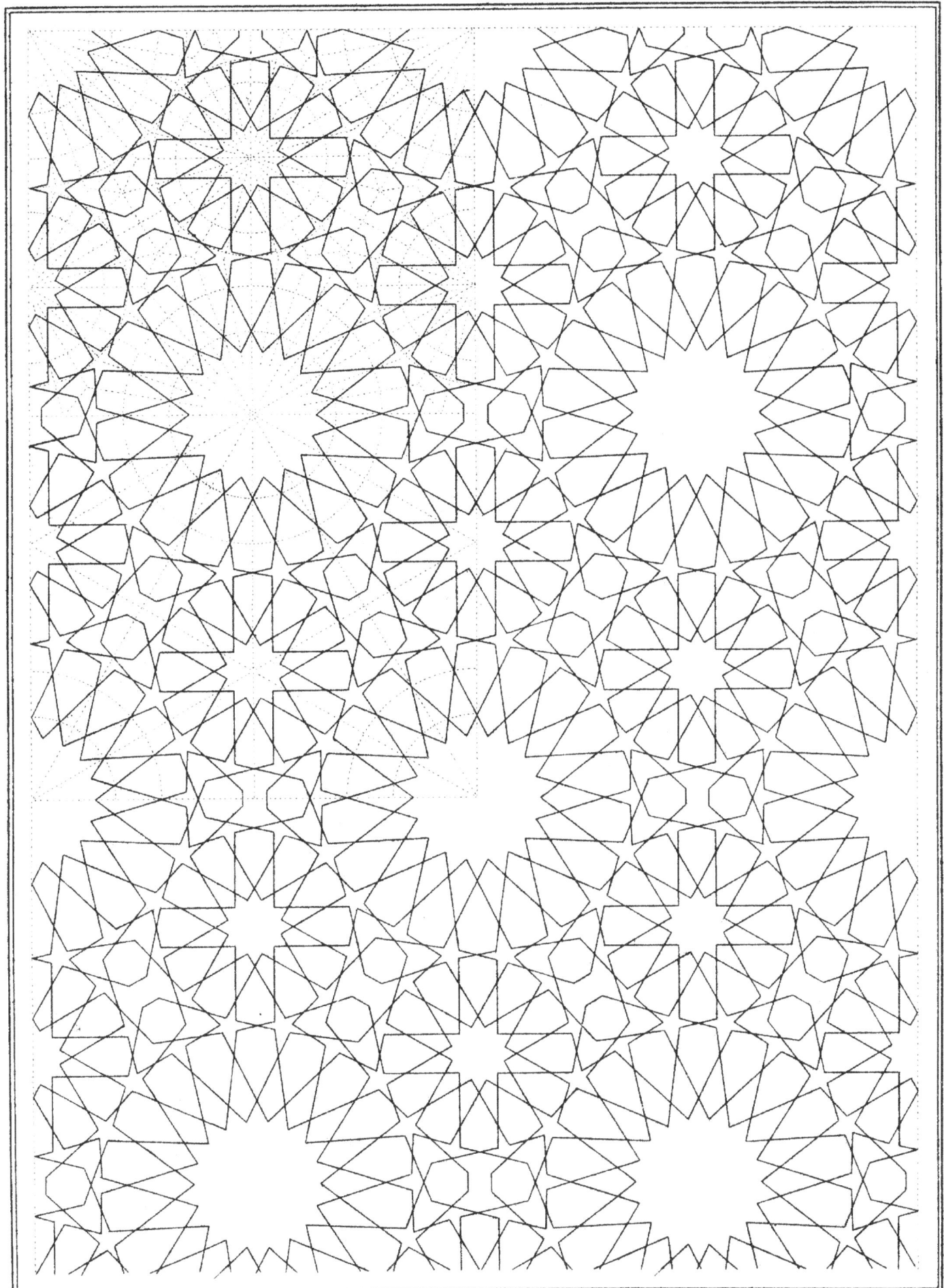

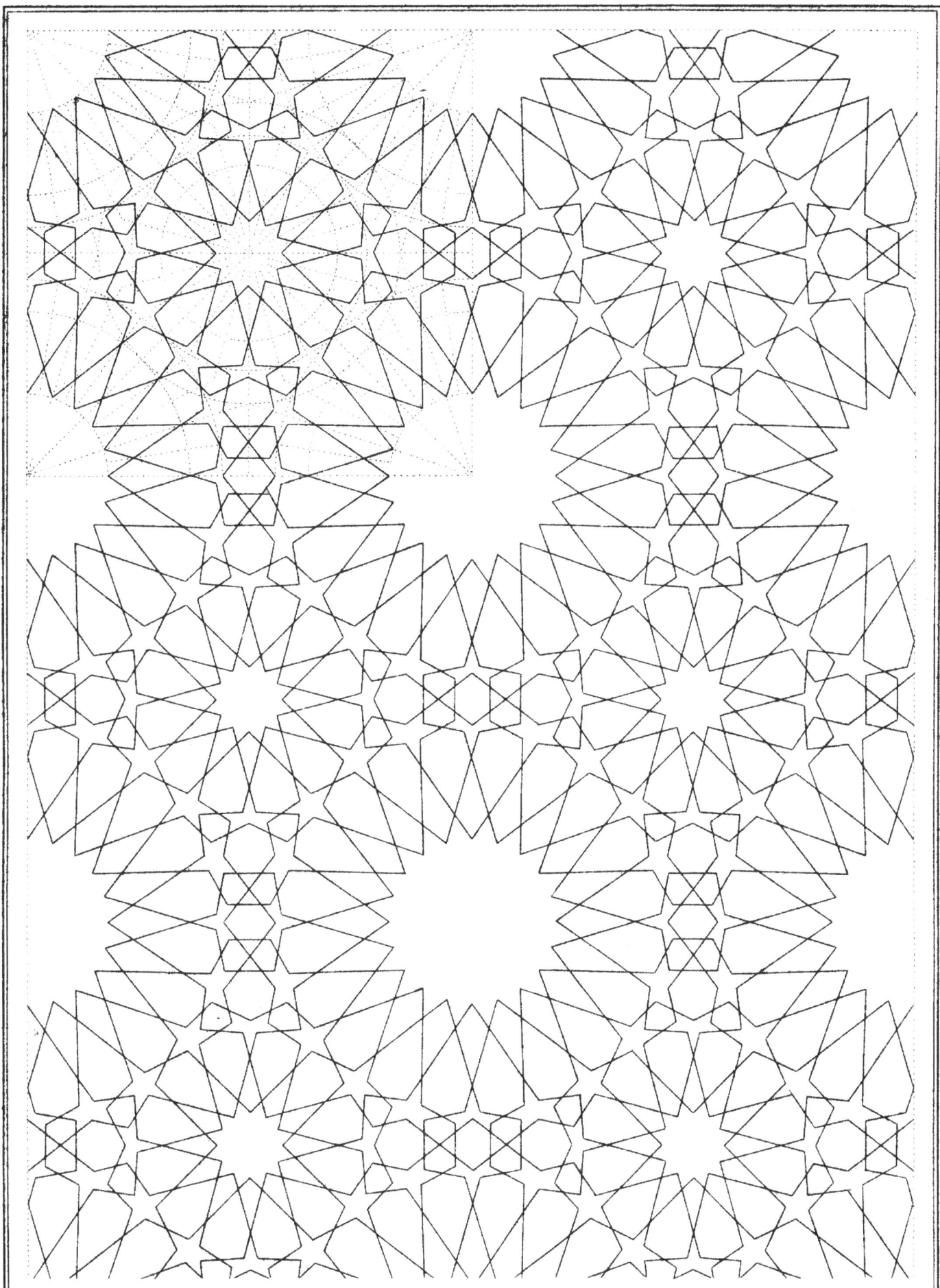

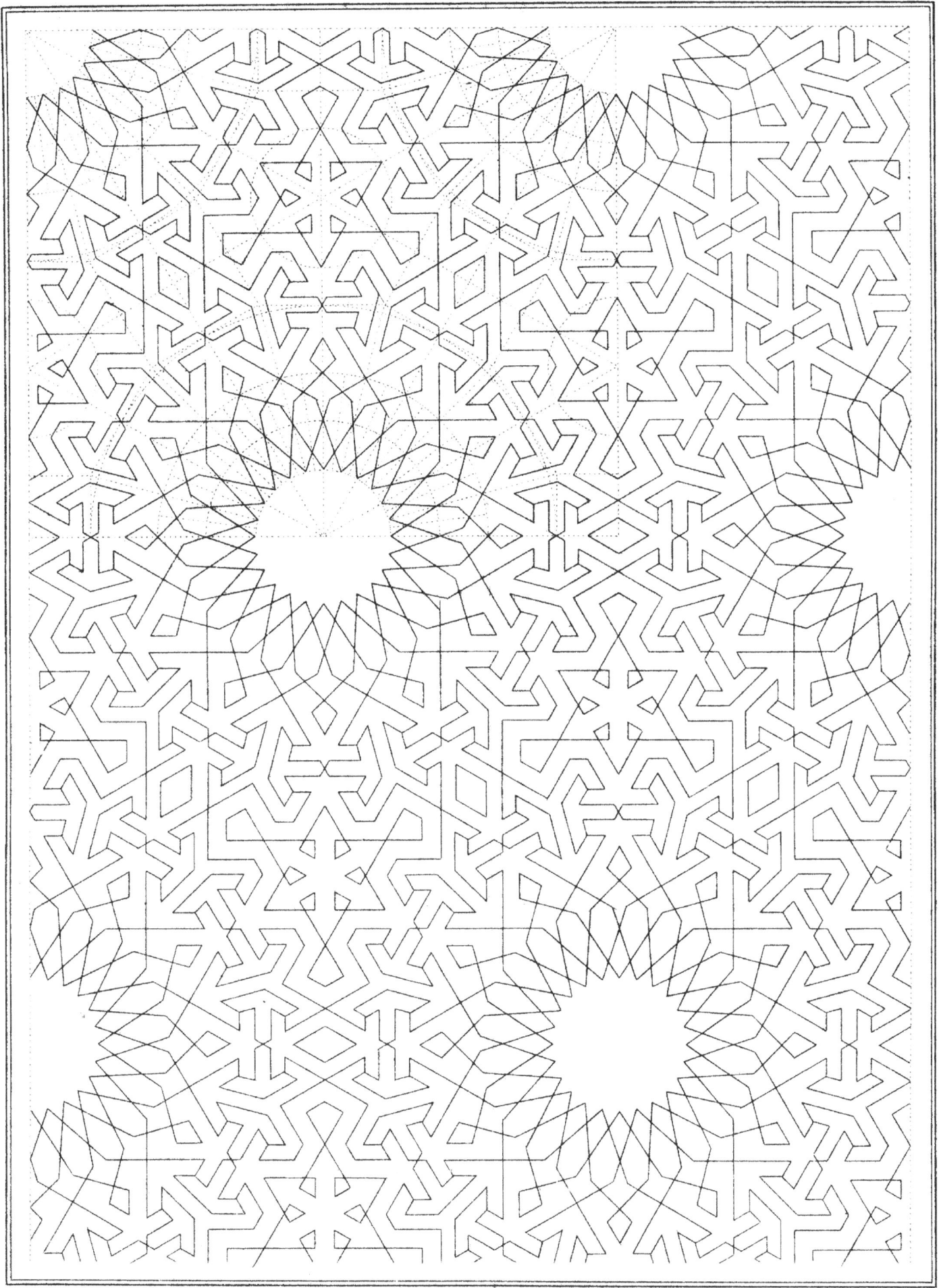

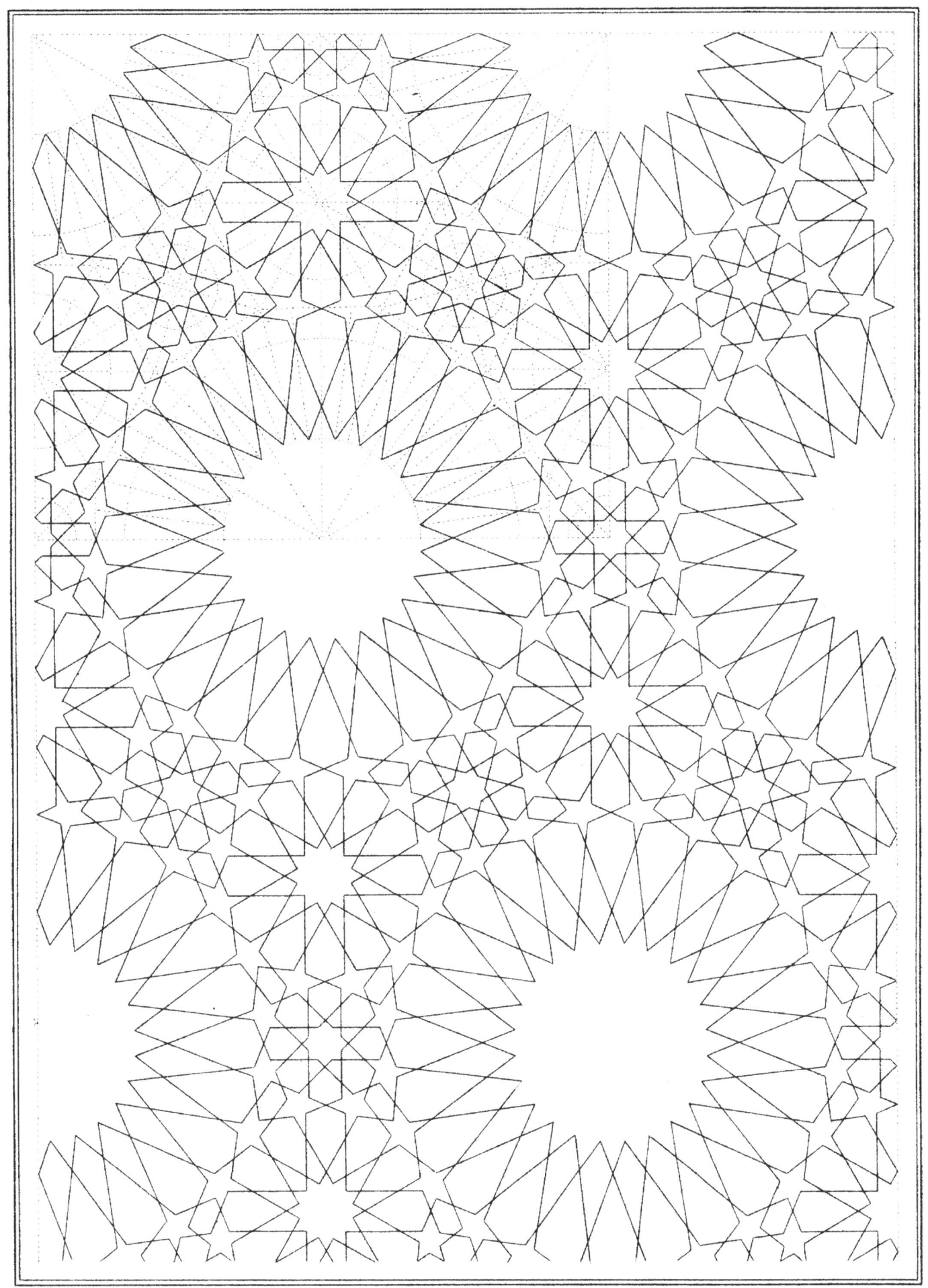

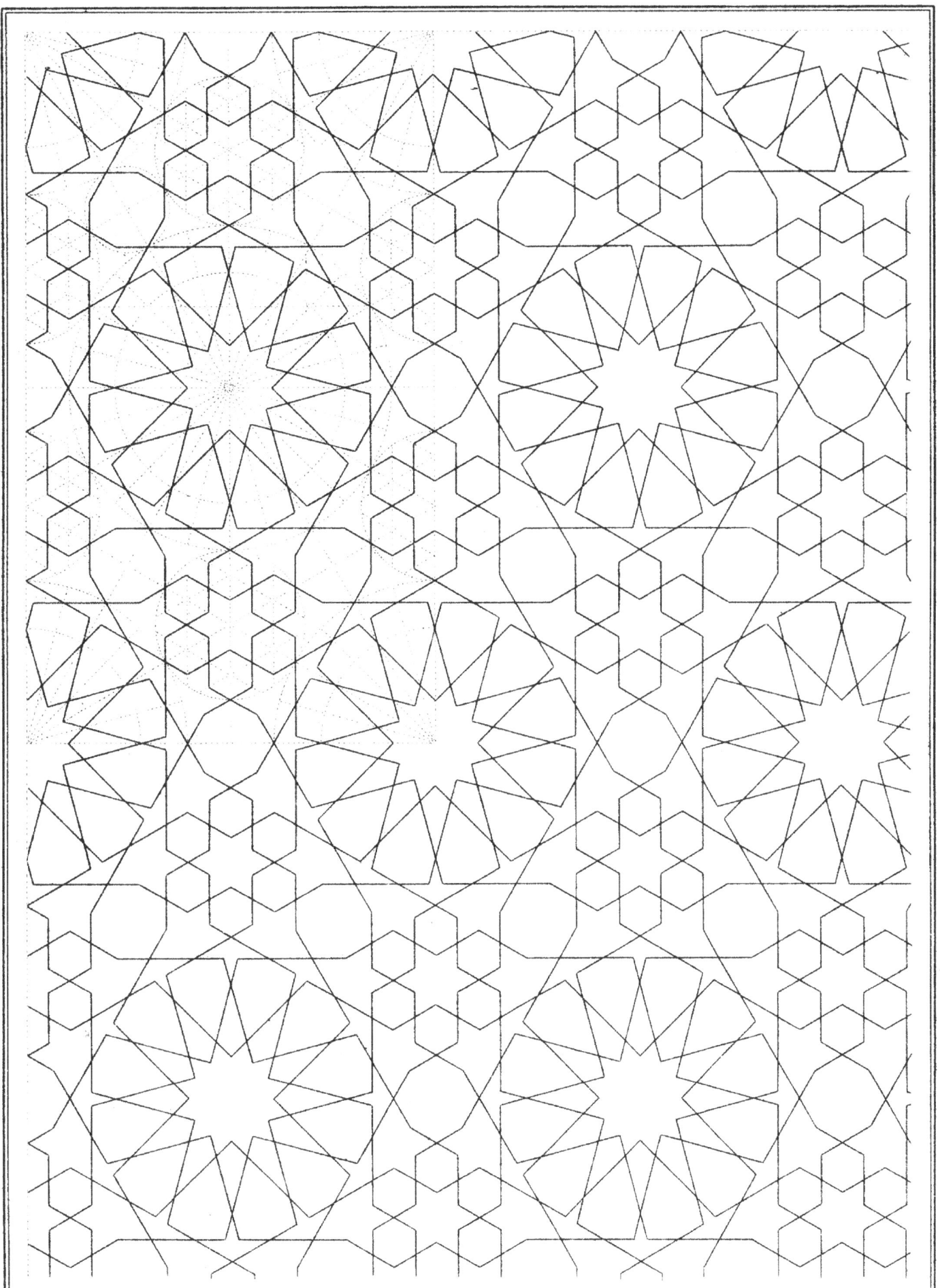

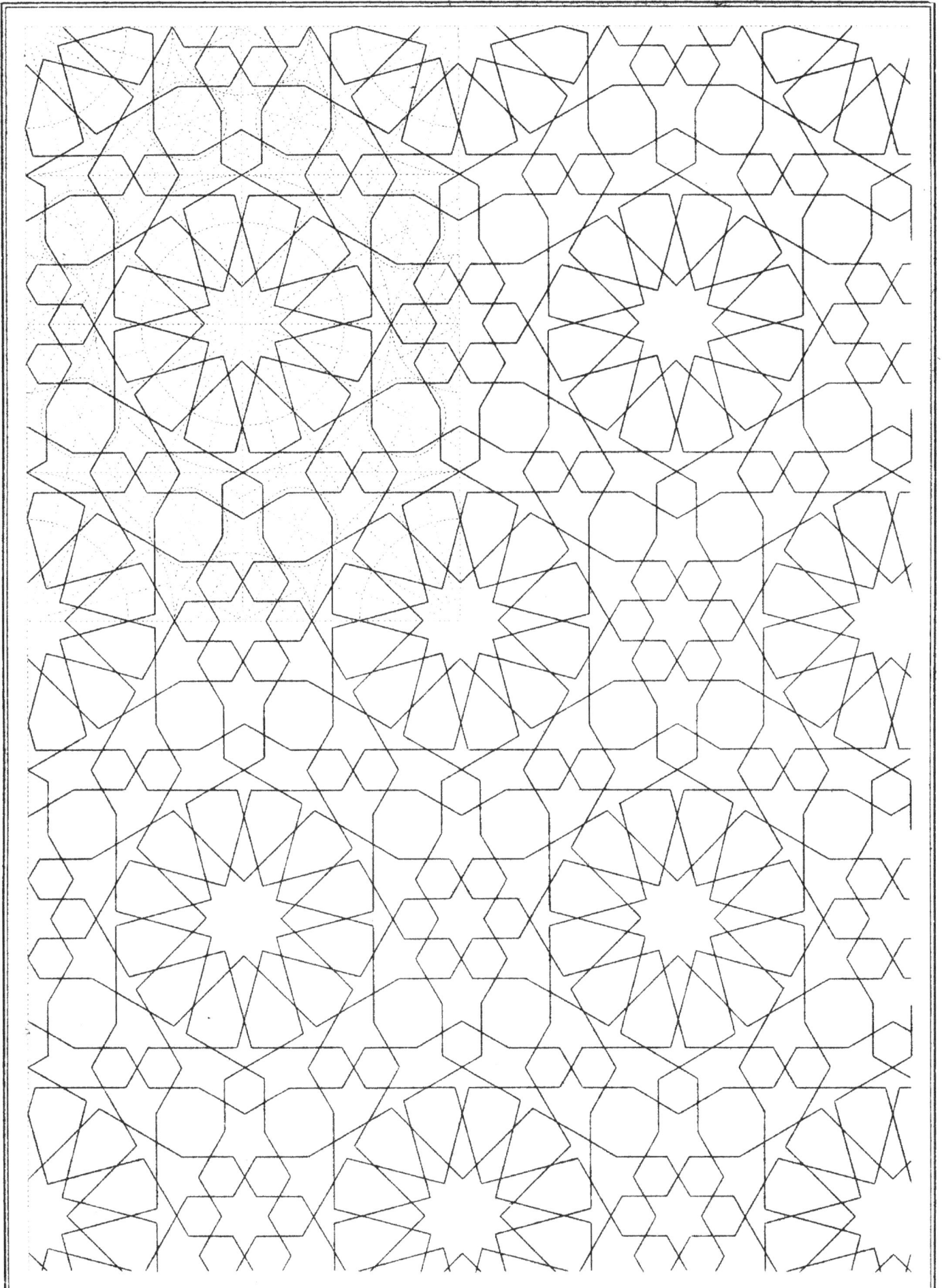

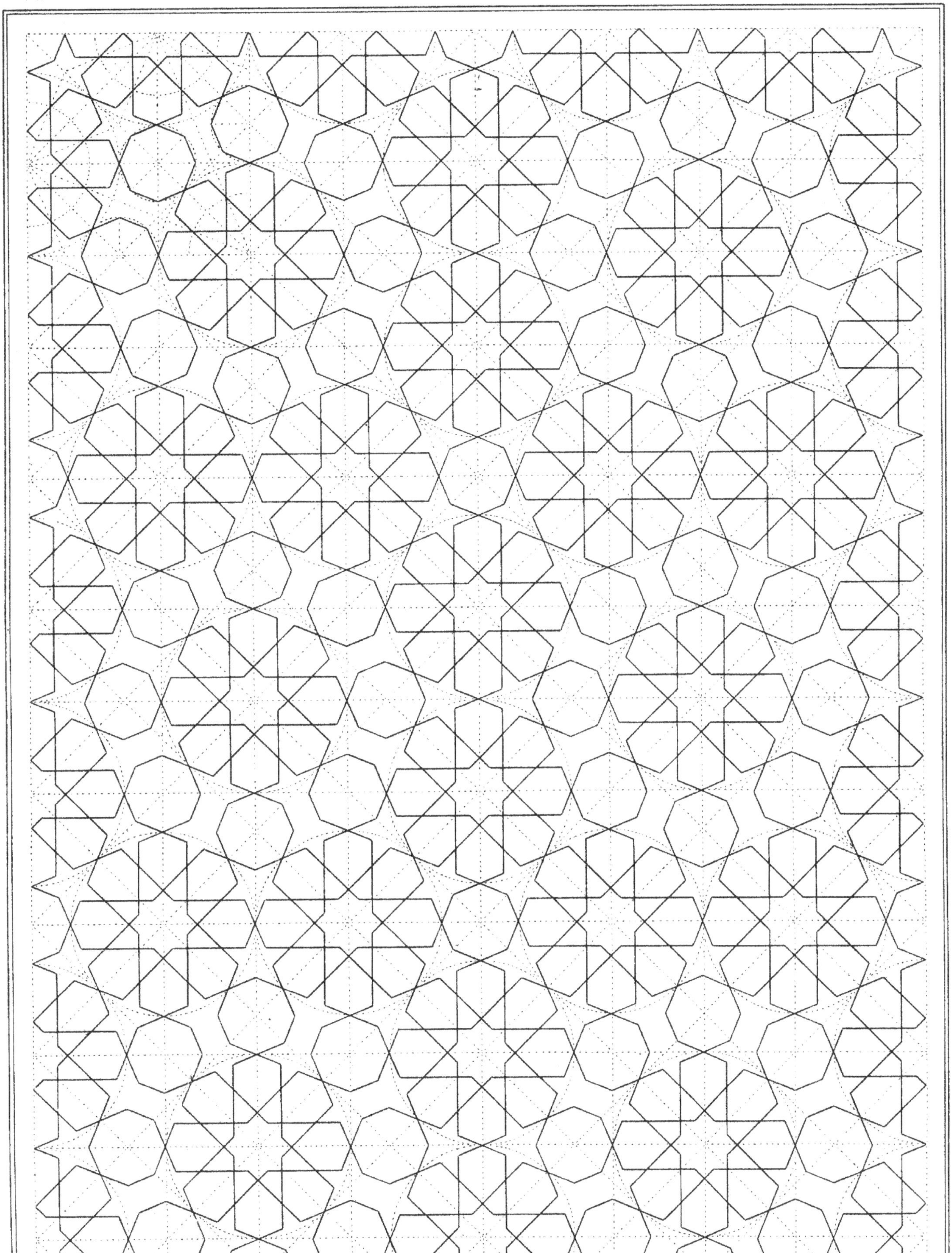

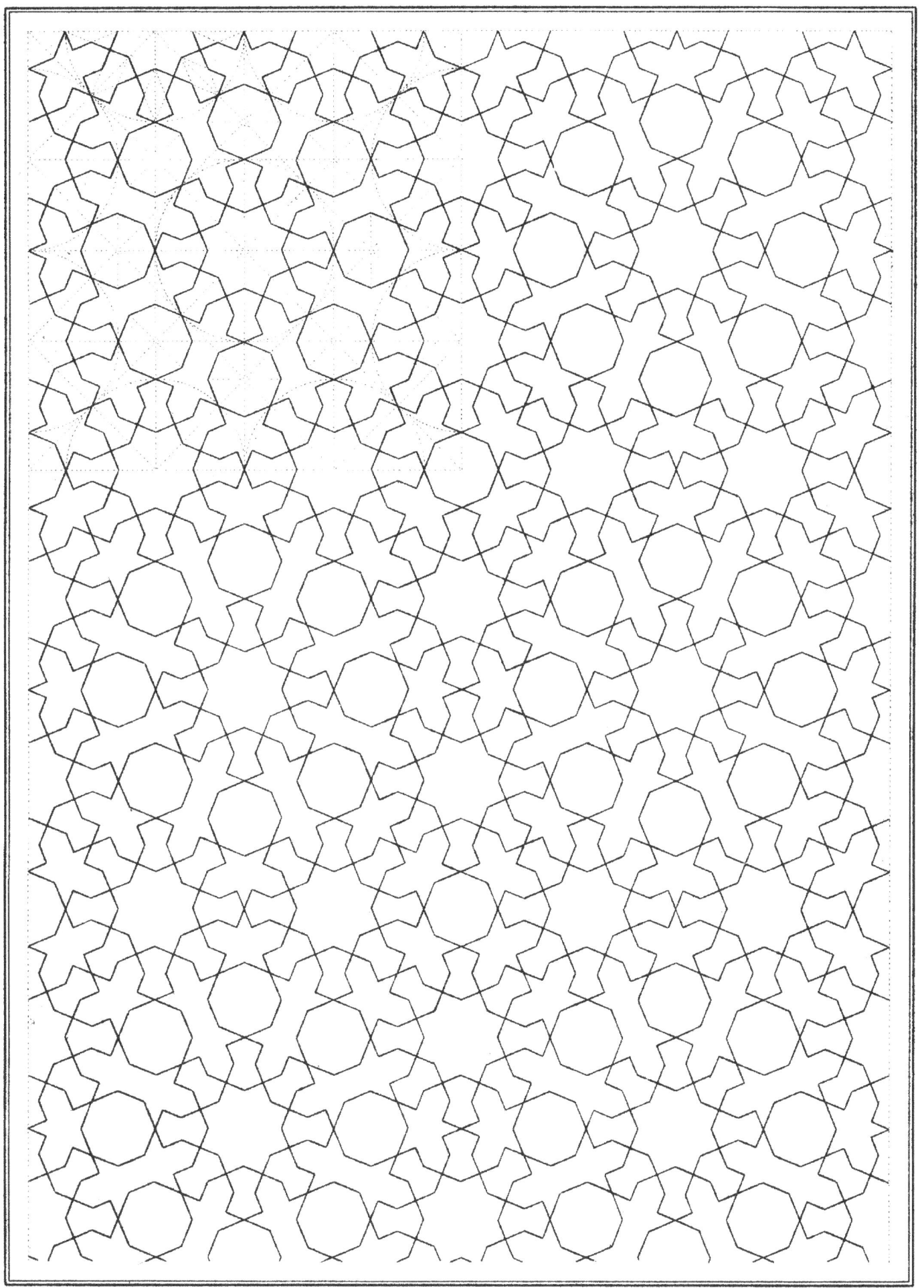

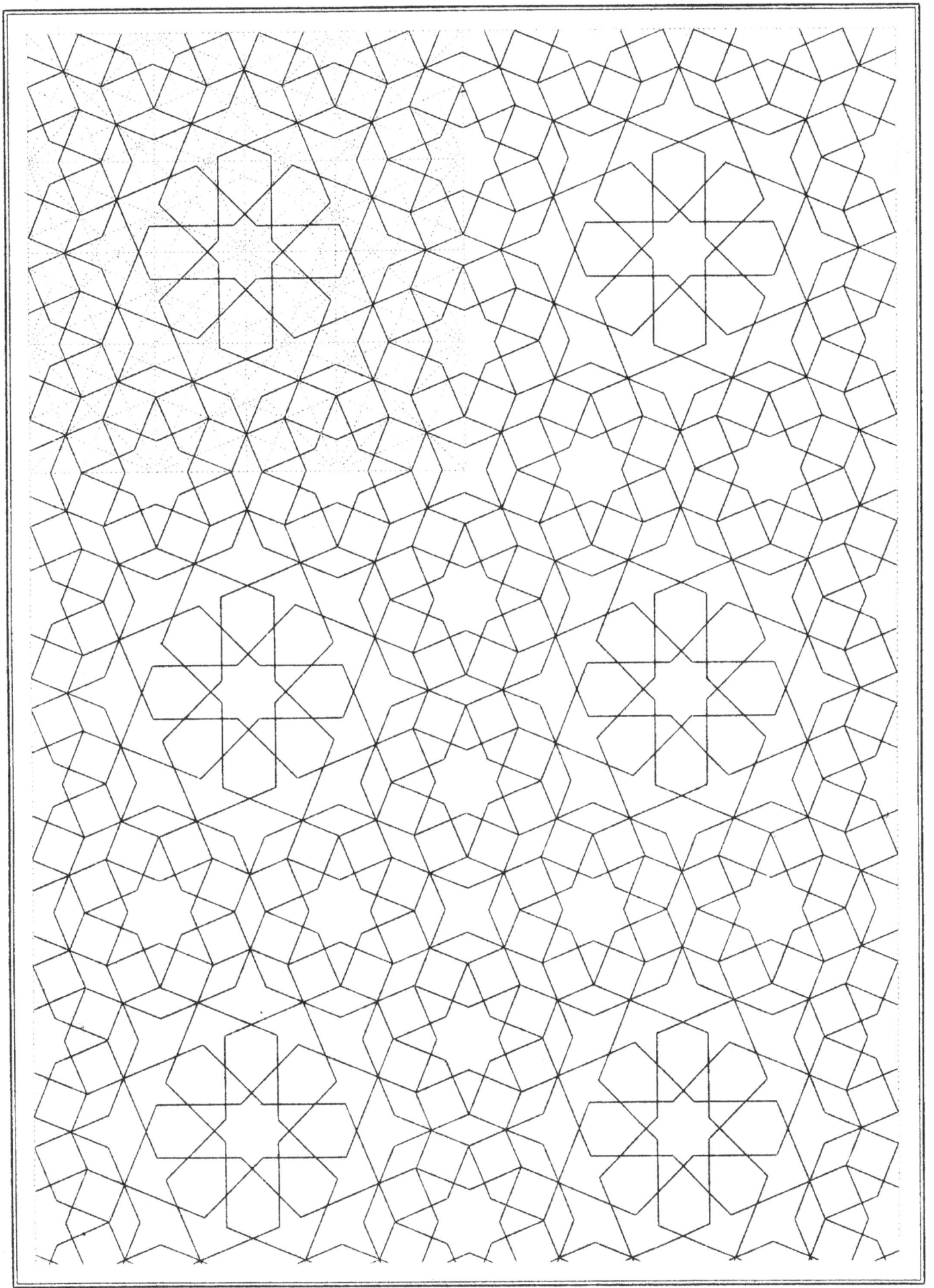

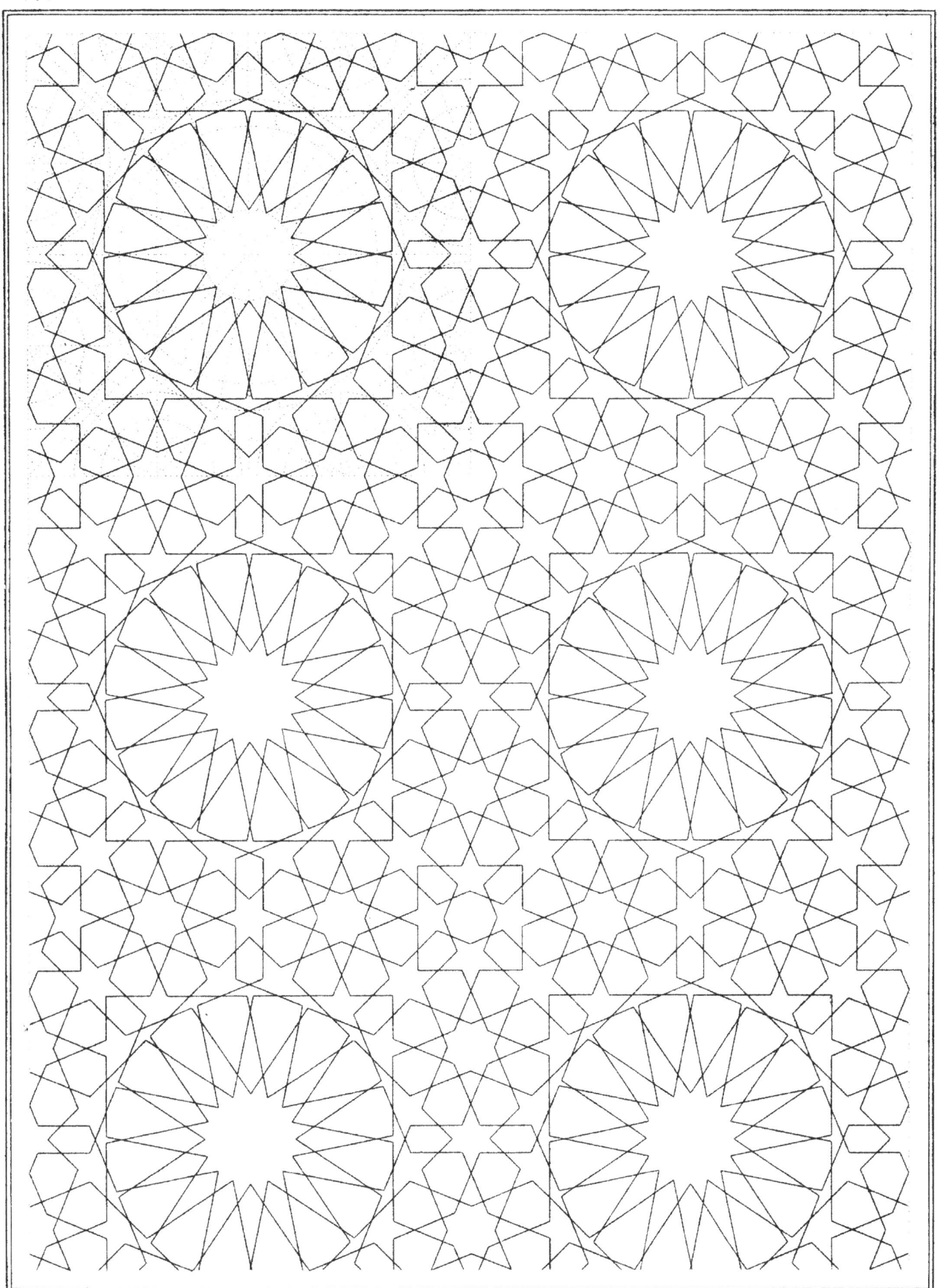

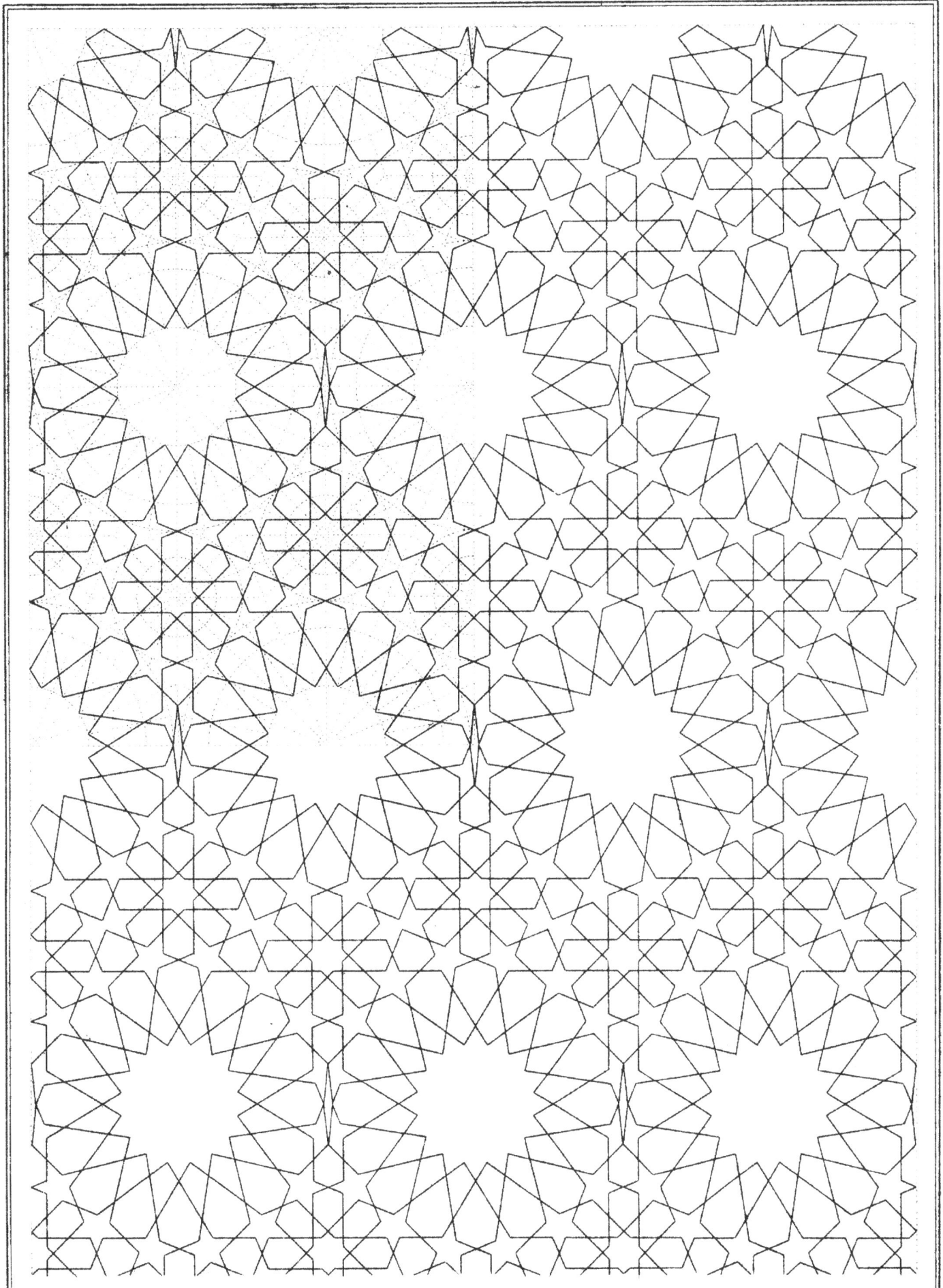

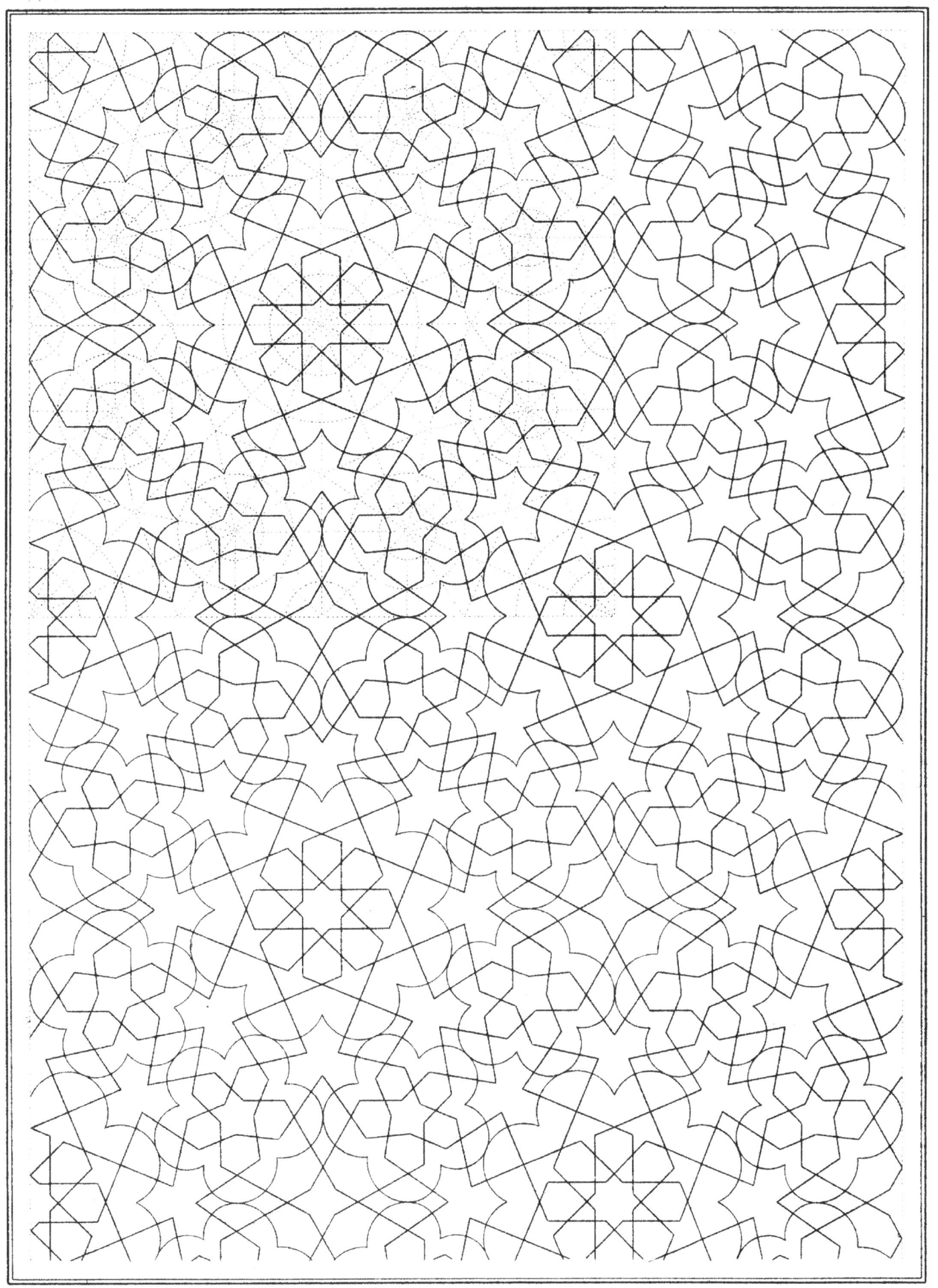

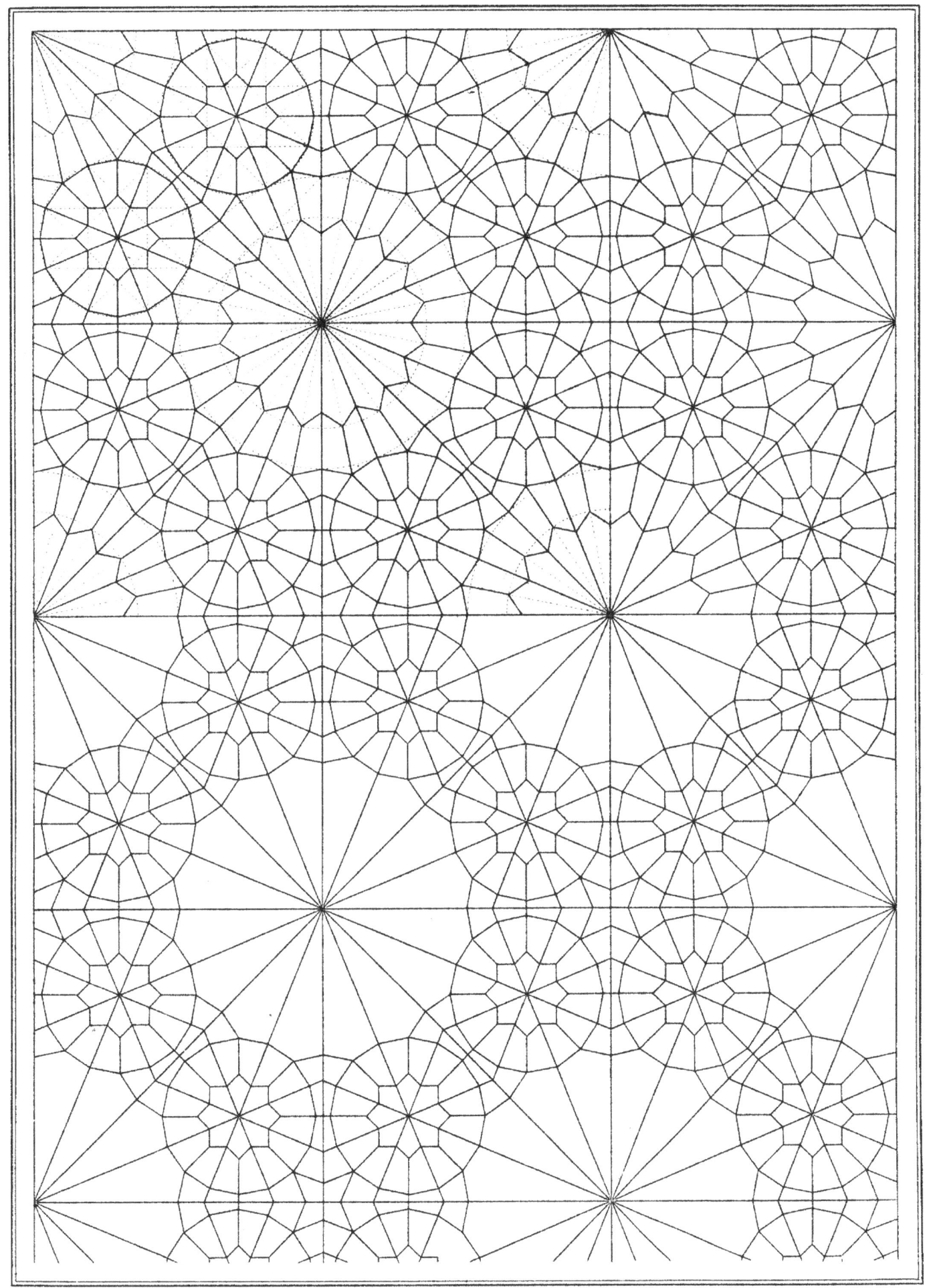

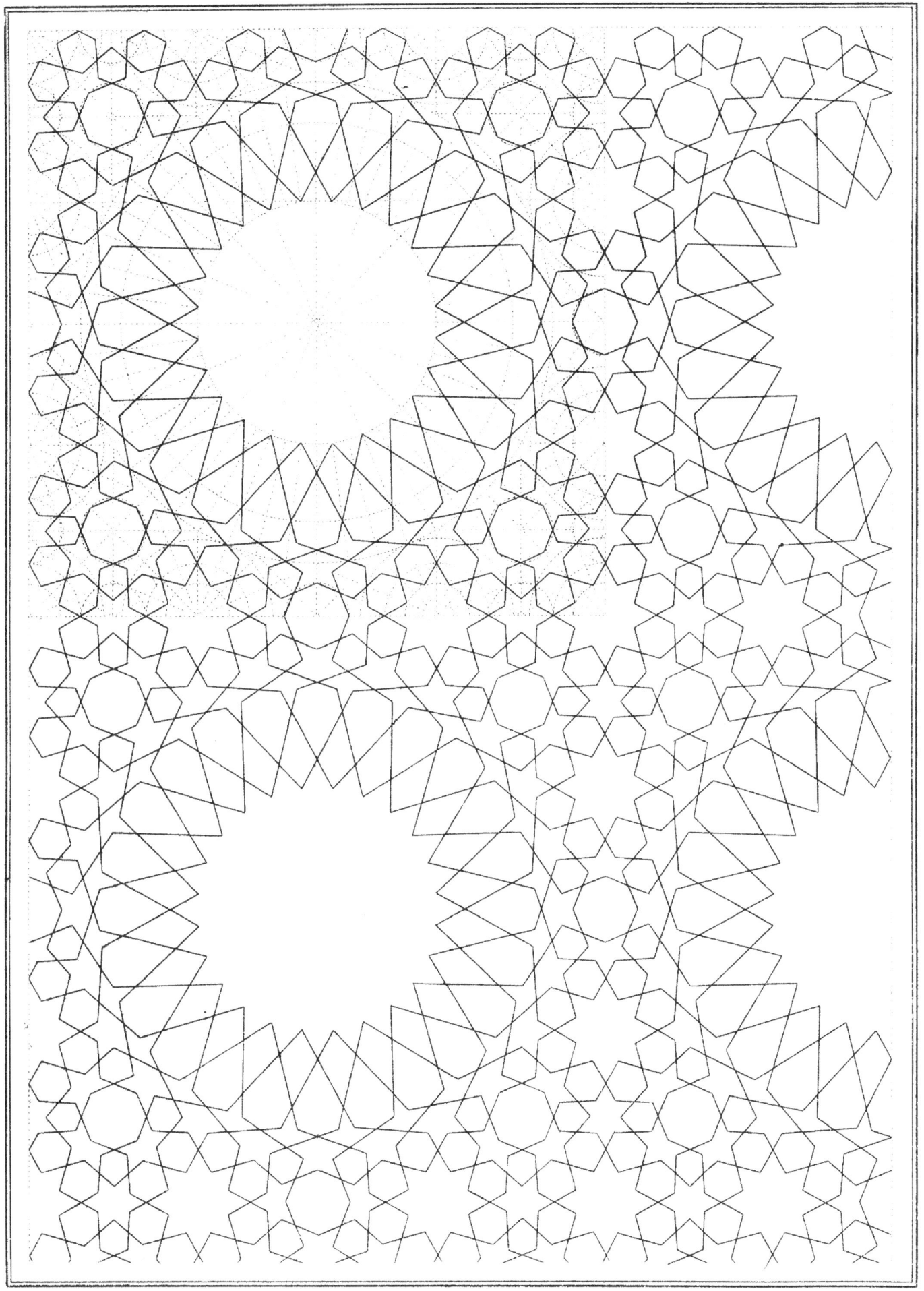

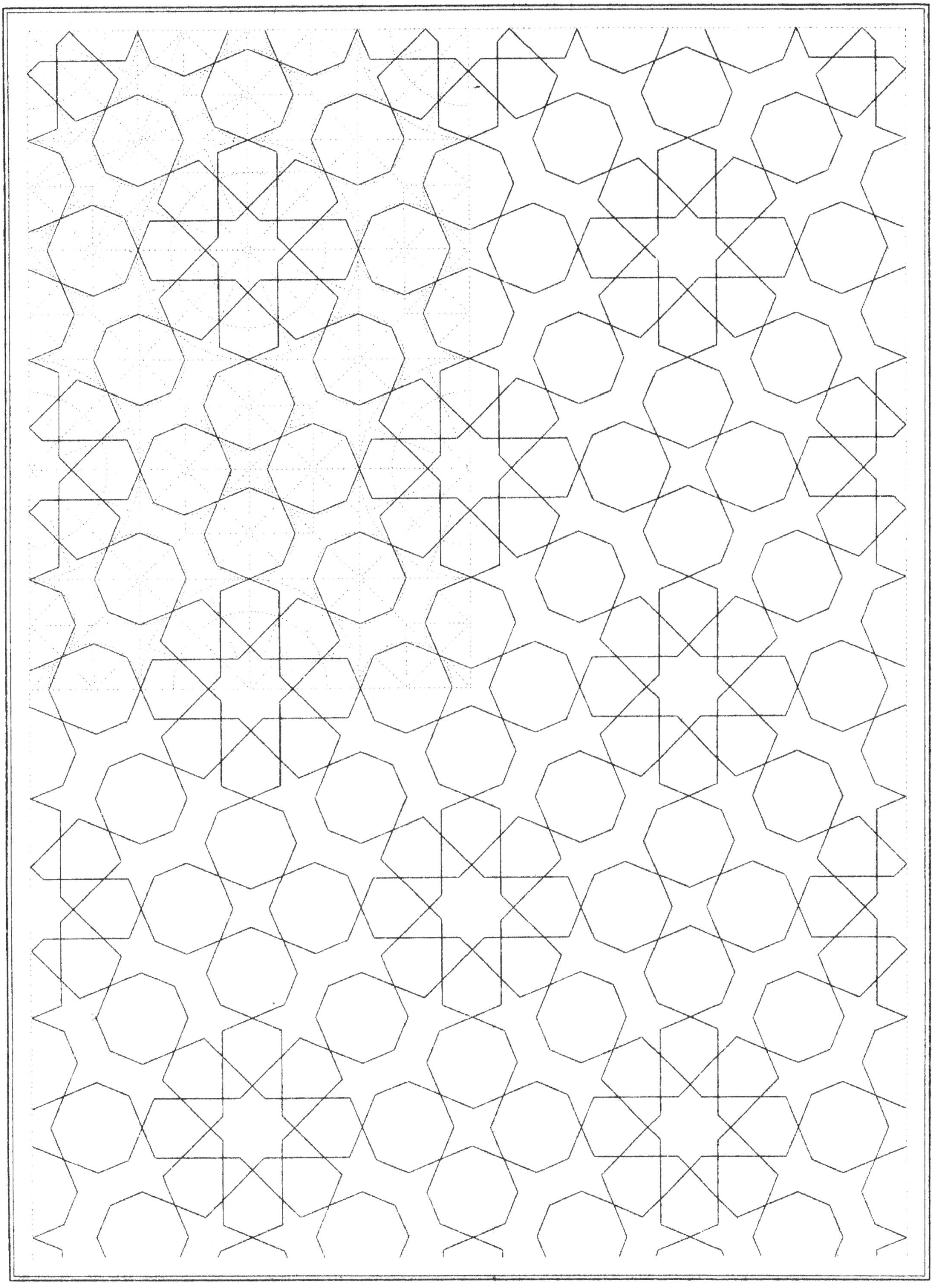

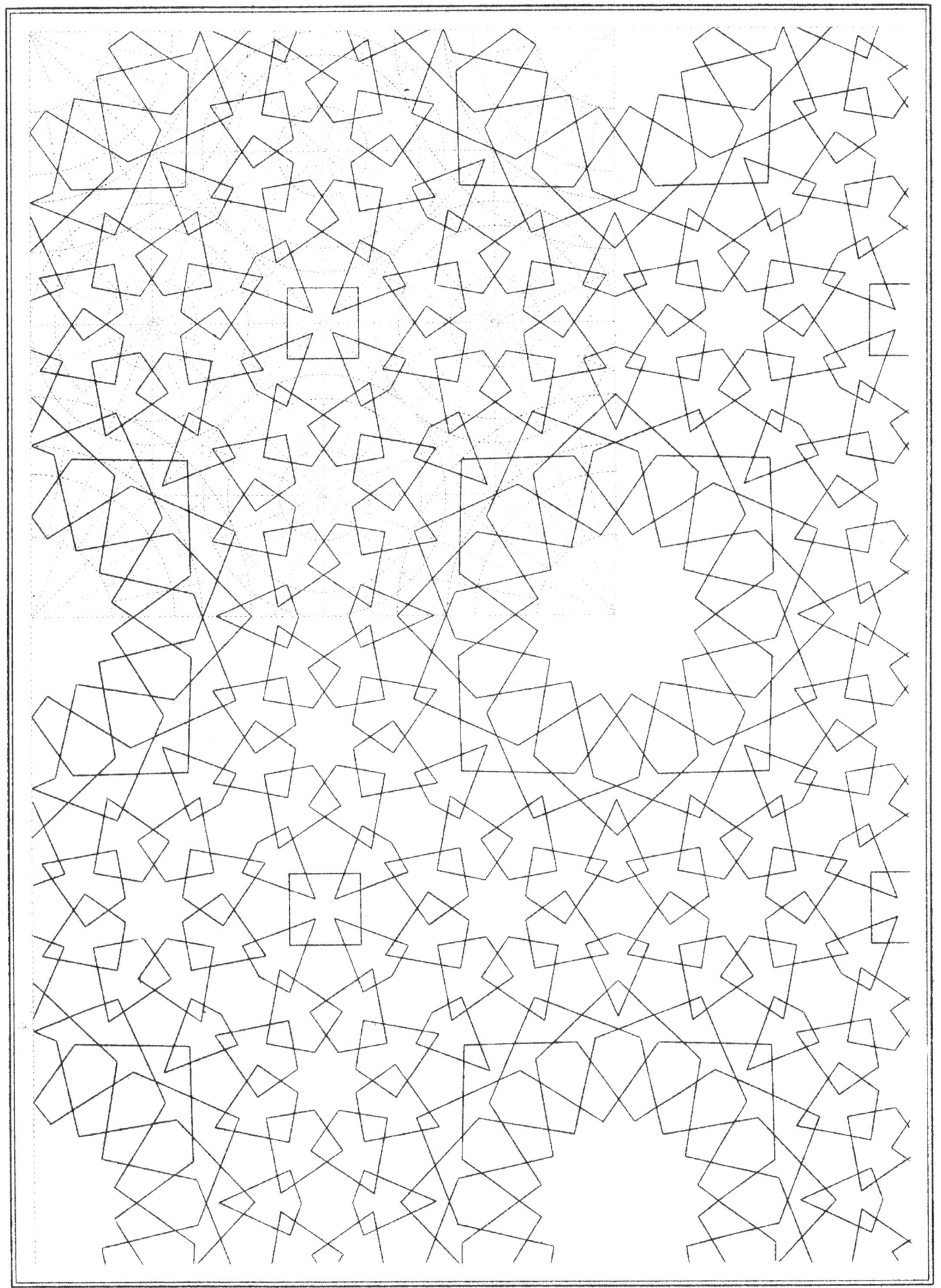

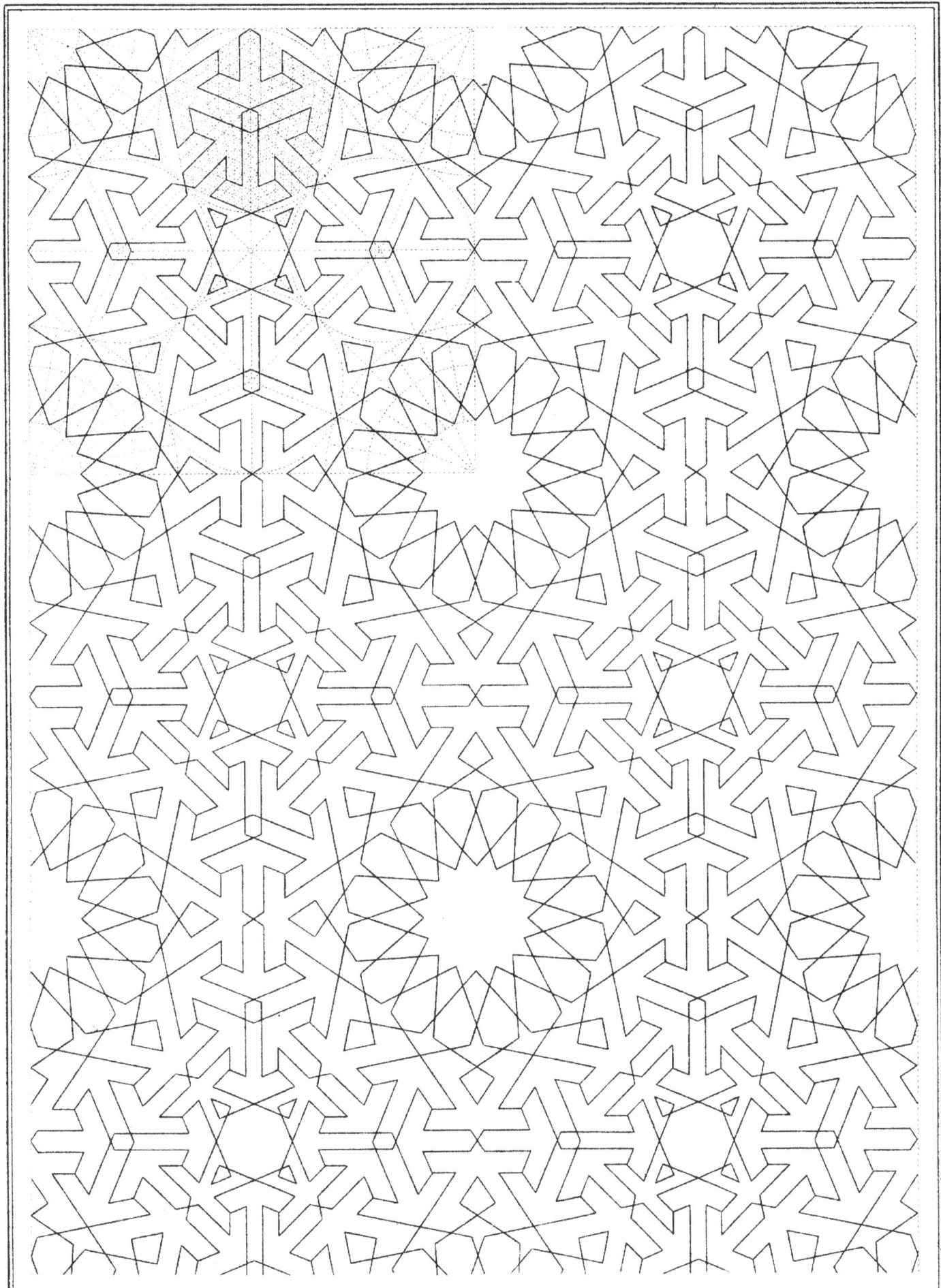

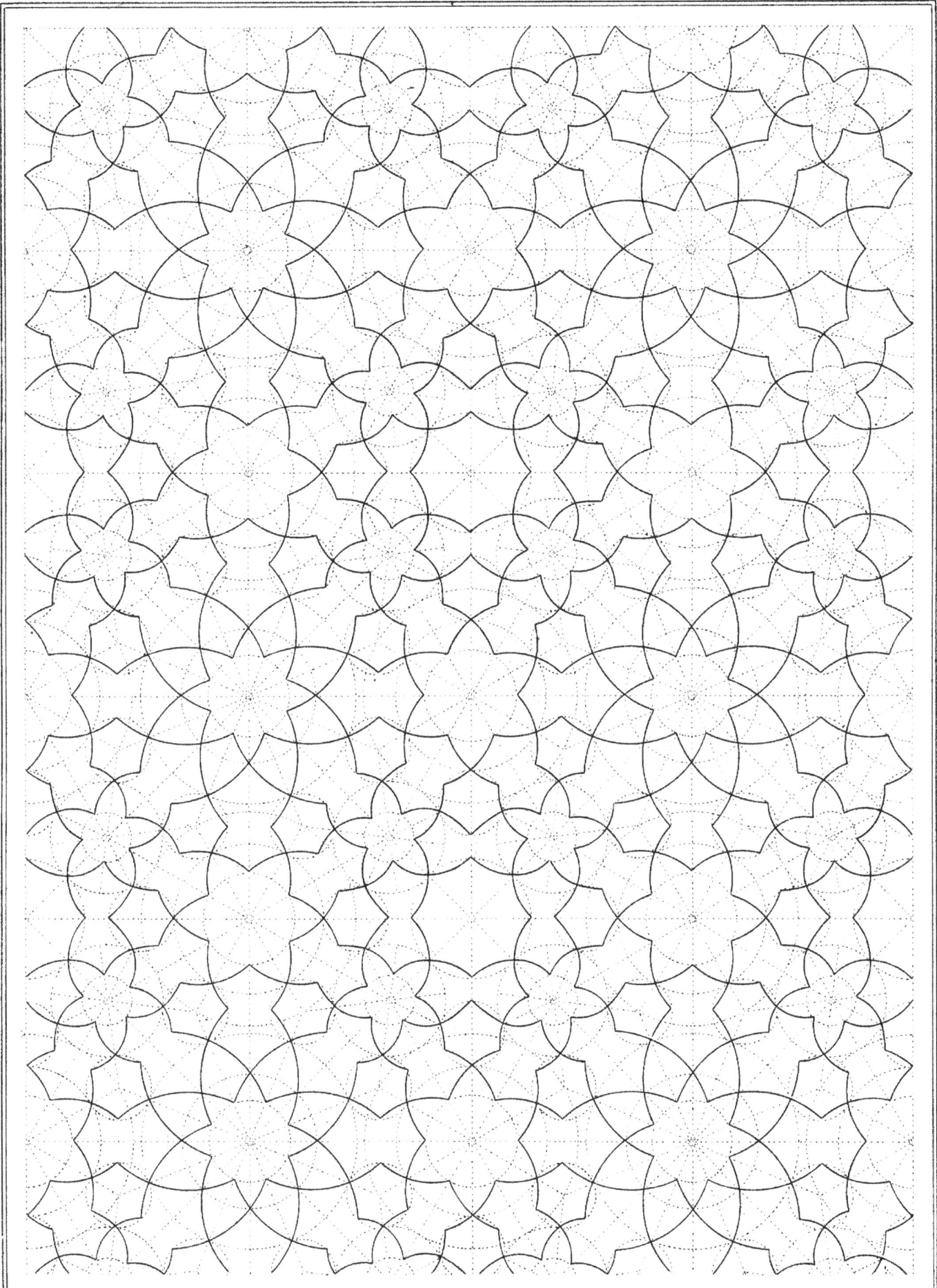

# BONUS

# Hexagon Paper Game

This is a short game, having a maximum of 15 moves and the game can never end in a tie. It is intended to be a game for two players.

Each player should select a different colored pen or pencil.

Players take it in turns to connect two dots.

The goal is to avoid completing a triangle with all three sides in your own color.

The first person to complete a triangle in their color loses.

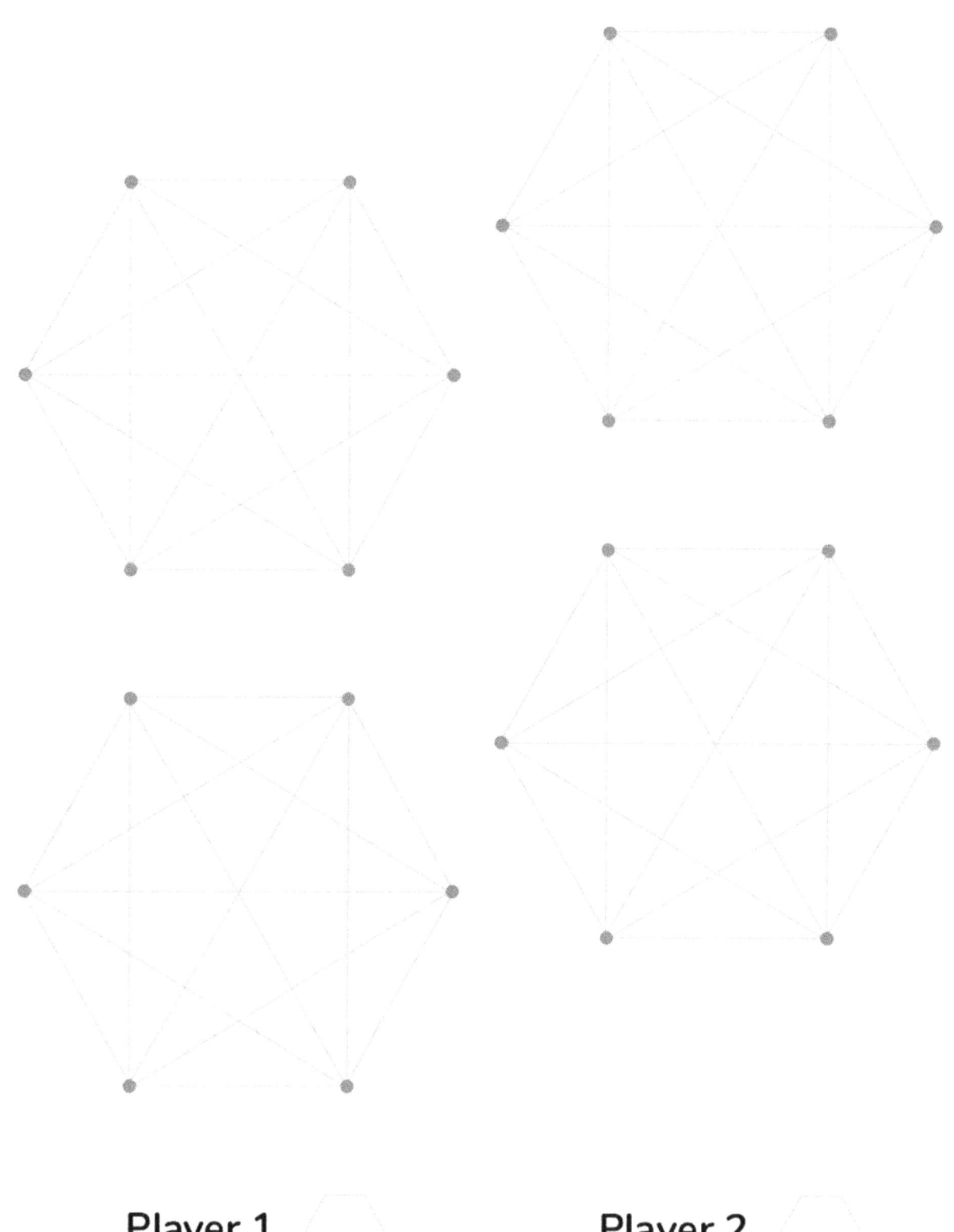

Player 1　　　　　　　　Player 2

Player 1

Player 2

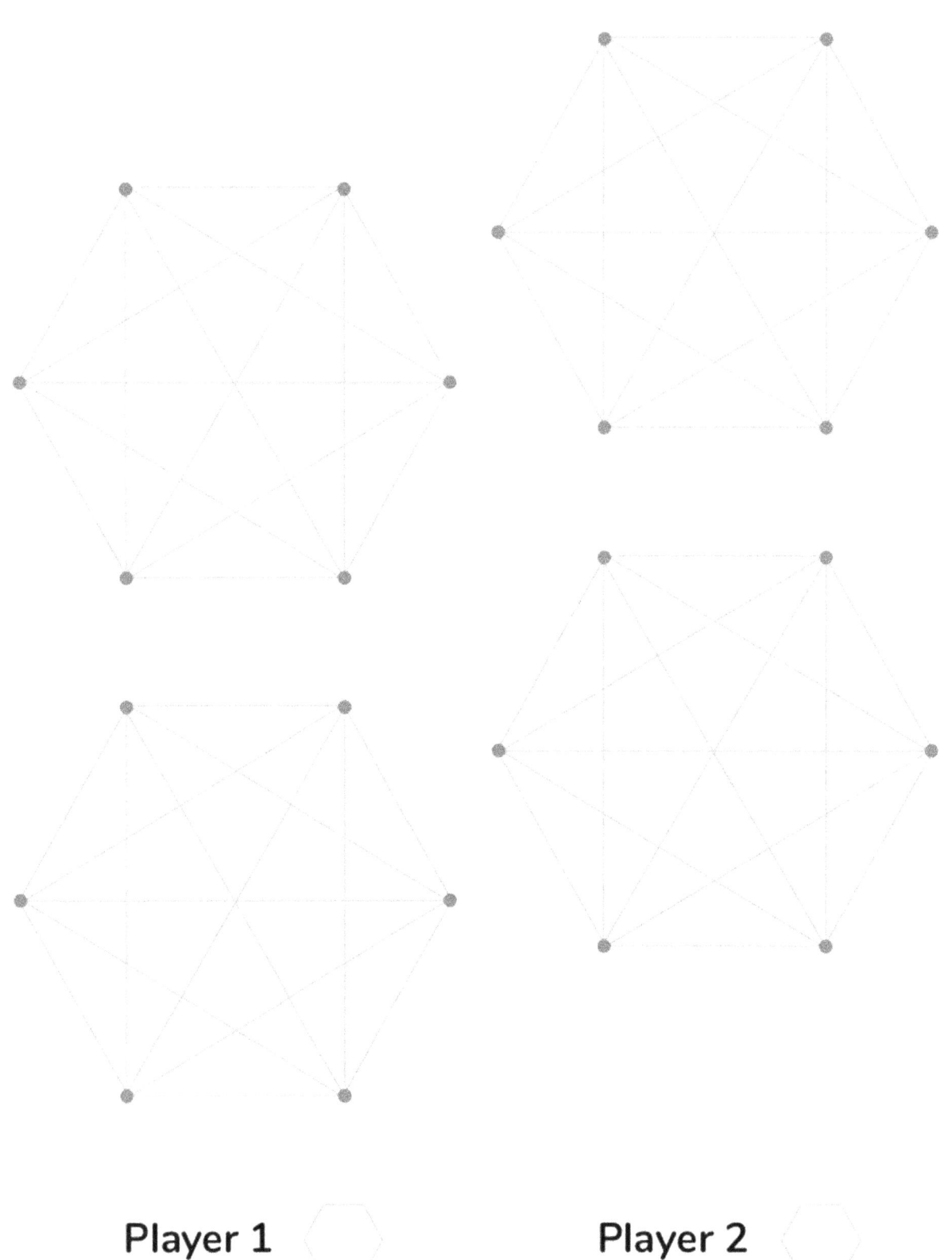

Player 1          Player 2

Player 1

Player 2

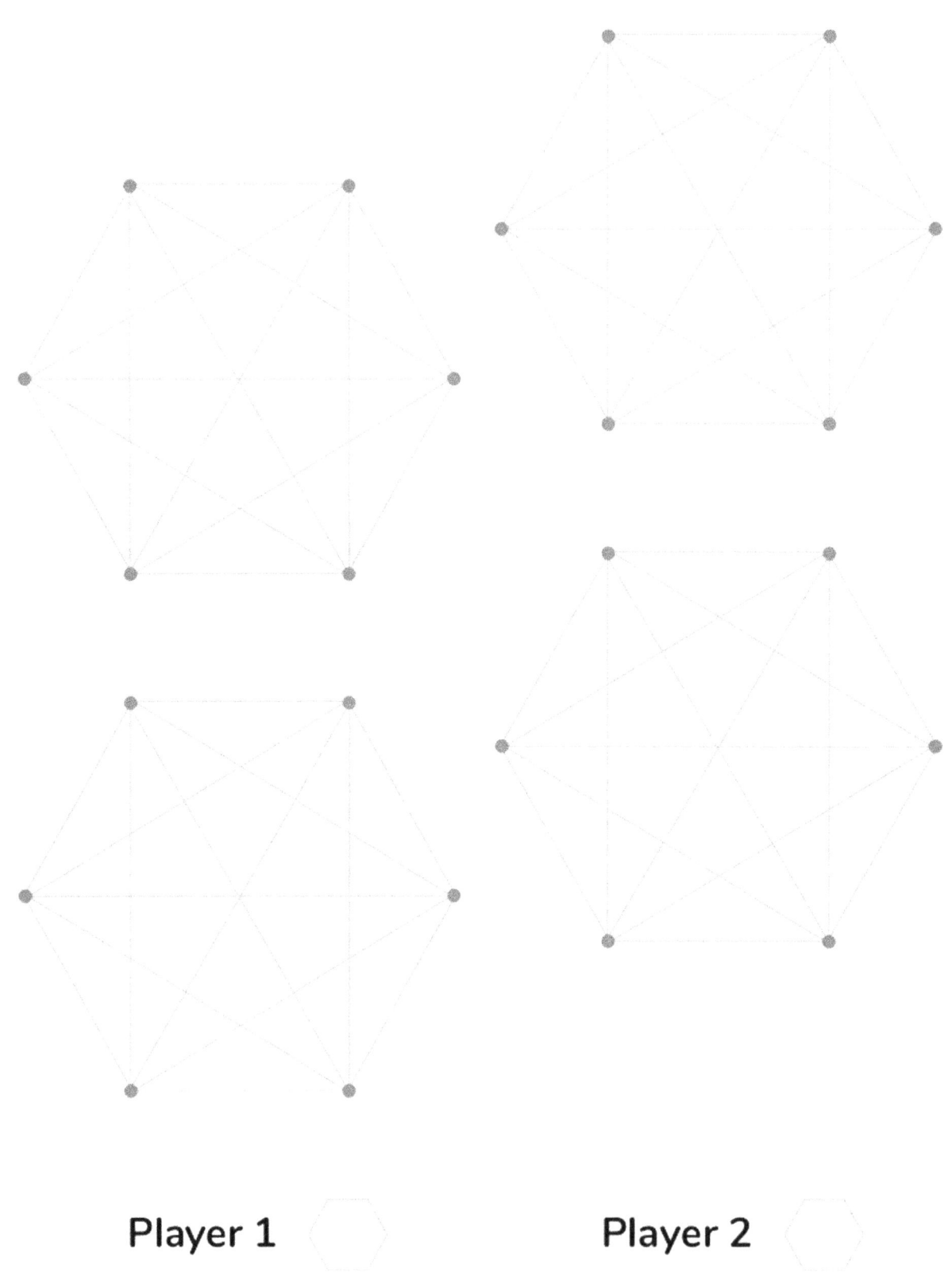

Player 1                    Player 2

Player 1

Player 2

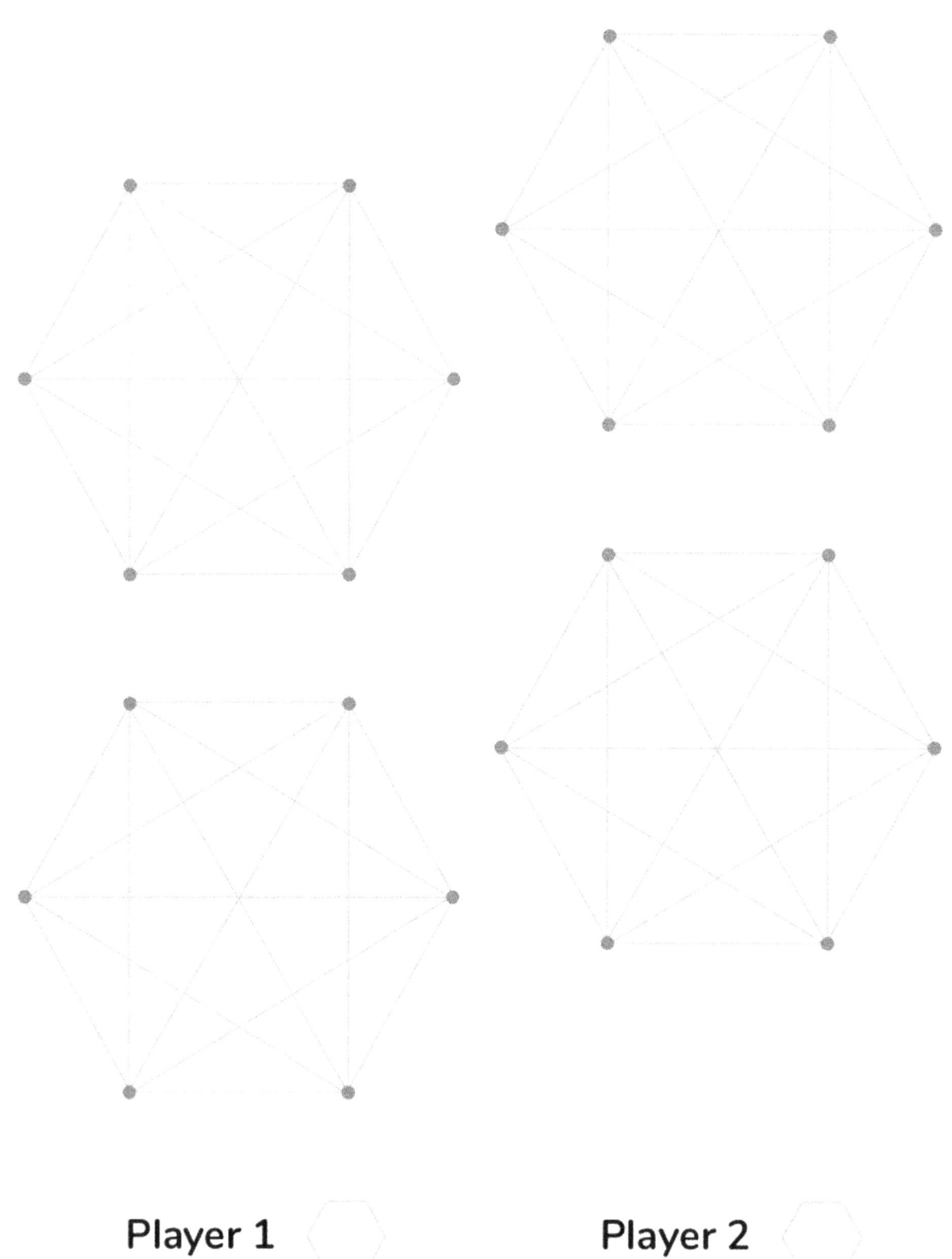

Player 1

Player 2

Player 1

Player 2

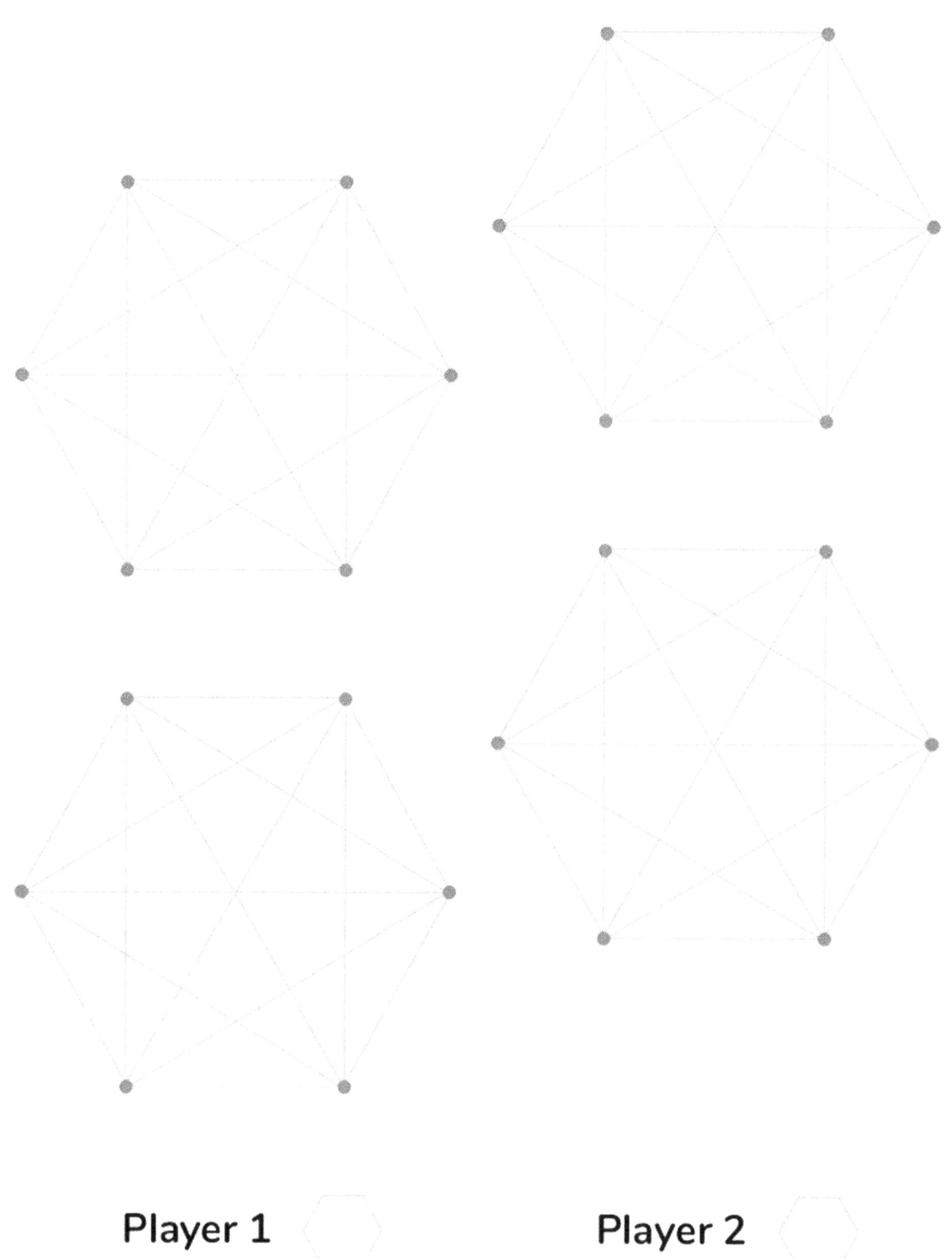

Player 1

Player 2

Player 1

Player 2

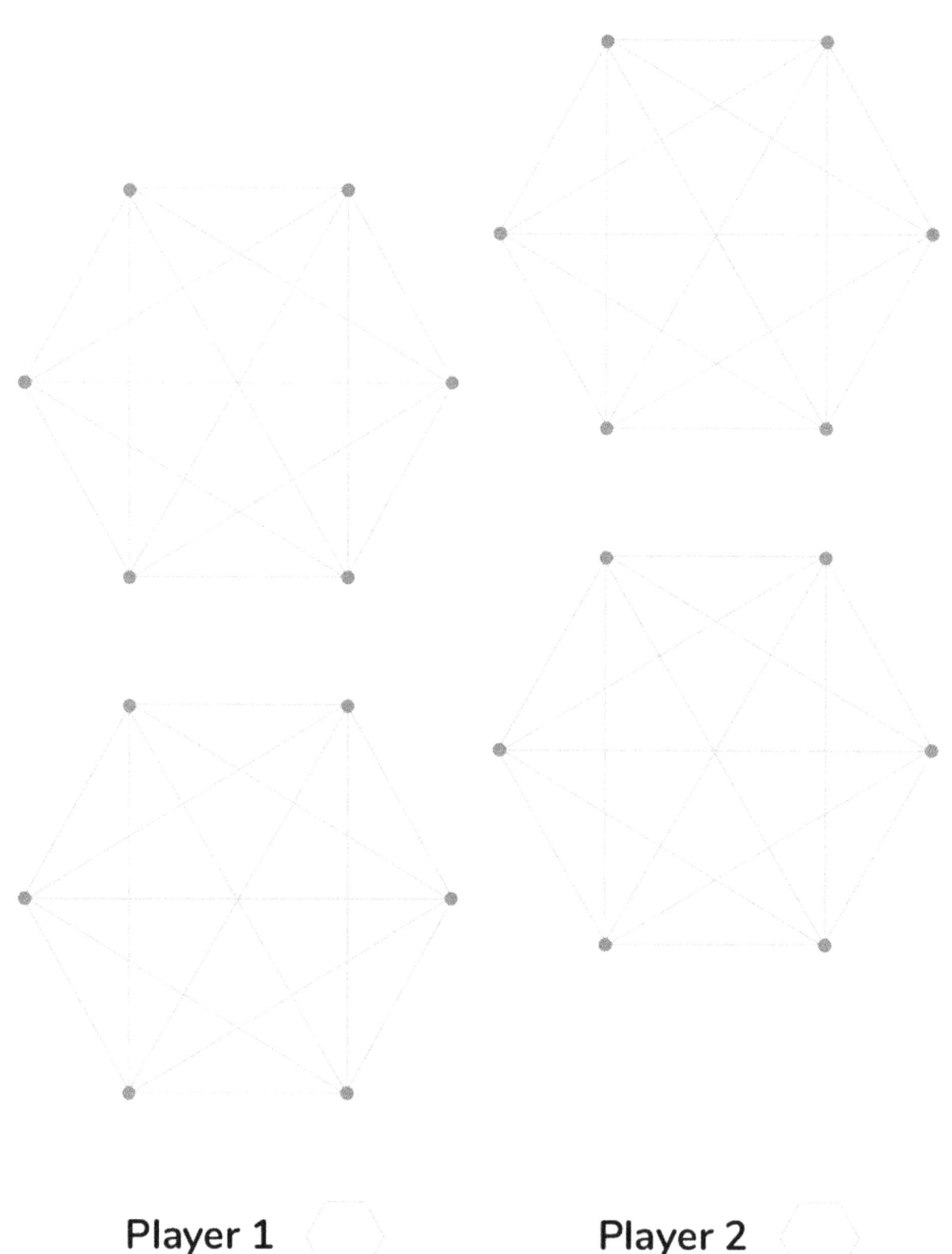

Player 1     Player 2

Player 1

Player 2